Guide

Sephardi Museum
TOLEDO

Edition prepared by:

Ana María López Álvarez

Santiago Palomero Plaza

María Luisa Menéndez Robles

The Synagogue of El Tránsito

The Museum wishes to thank the following for their collaboration
with the scientific advisory team on the new layout:

Consultants
D. Jacob Hassán, CSIC
D. José Luis Lacave Riaño, CSIC
Dña. Encarnación Marín Padilla, CSIC
D. Emiliano Martínez Borobio, CSIC
Dña. Yolanda Moreno Koch, Univ. Complutense
D. Ángel Sáenz-Badillos, Univ. Complutense

Consultants for Toledo
D. José Aguado Villalba, RABA y CH de Toledo
D. Ricardo Izquierdo Benito, Univ. de Castilla La Mancha
D. Antonio de Juan, Escuela taller de Alarcos, Ciudad Real
Dña. Pilar León Tello, AHN
D. Julio Porres Martín-Cleto, RABA y CH de Toledo

Legal Deposit: M-3863-1998
I.S.B.N. 84-8003-082-8

Design: *Alberto Caffaratto*
Layout: *Marina Caffaratto*
Photographs: *Museo Sefardí (Ministerio de Educación y Cultura) M.A. Otero*

Photomechanical production: *Lucam*

Translation: Nigel Williams

Front cover illustration: Synagogue of El Tránsito, Interior
Printed by: *Estudios Gráficos Europeos*

Impreso en España, Printed in Spain.

CONTENTS

THE SYNAGOGUE OF EL TRÁNSITO

History and background

The synagogue of Samuel Halevi was built between 1336 and 1357 on the orders of Samuel Halevi Abulafia, who held various posts - High Court Judge, Diplomat and Royal Treasurer – at the court of Peter I of Castile.

Despite the vicissitudes suffered by the Jews of Toledo, the Synagogue was never affected, even during the destruction of part of the Jewish quarter in 1391.

After the expulsion of the Jews in 1492, the Catholic Kings delivered to the Order of Calatrava: "The great synagogue which the Jews had in Toledo in exchange for the fortress and palaces of Galiana with their church of the Santa Fe, which were possessions of this order".

After 1494 the building was no longer used as a synagogue and became part of the priory of San Benito, with the area formerly occupied by the rabbinical school and the women's gallery serving as a hospital and home for the knights of Calatrava. The large old prayer room, referred to in records as the church of San Benito, became a Christian place of worship and a number of knights of the Order were buried there.

In the 16th century, what had been a hospital and home became a church only, and a door to the sacristy "with the Plateresque charm of the age" and an embedded arch, dedicated to the worship of the Virgin, were added. An altarpiece was installed next to the central body of the old *hekhal* and the main altar was placed on the original synagogue floor. The former women's gallery was probably walled in and used as a dwelling, and wooden floorboards were laid for the choir on the west side.

In the 17th century the church of San Benito became popularly known as *El Tránsito* when a Calatrava knight commissioned the painter Diego Correa (Madrid School) to paint a picture of *El Tránsito de Nuestra Señora* ("The Death of Our Lady"). The painting adorned the Plateresque altar thereafter. At this time the Archive of the Military Orders of Calatrava and Alcántara was built against the synagogue's north wall. This area now contains Rooms I, II and III of the Sephardi Museum.

In the 18th century the decline of the military orders also affected the hitherto rich church of Nuestra Señora del Tránsito, which contemporary records by then referred to simply as a chapel. A drawing of the old synagogue by Palomares includes its original

Previous page: View of Toledo.

Exterior of the Synagogue of El Tránsito.

An engraving.

façade and balconies, a belfry and the chaplain's dwelling.
The sorry state of the archive and the need for repairs are mentioned in documents written throughout the century.
During the Napoleonic Wars the building was used as a barracks and continued to deteriorate throughout the rest of the 19th century, remaining a chapel until the Disentailment. On 1st May 1877, it was declared a "National Monument" and a number of restoration programmes were carried out to remedy its bad state of repair.
In 1910 the old synagogue was entrusted to the Board of the El Greco Museum, chaired by the Marquis of la Vega-Inclán, who restored it in accordance with the criteria of the times.
Between 1910 and 1968 the synagogue came under the protection and custody of the Vega-Inclán Foundations, the last restoration work being carried out in the 1960s: the old choir stalls, which had been added during the Marquis's time, were removed, as were the gravestones of the knights of Calatrava; the stuccowork and the wooden floors were repaired; and tapestries and silk, a gift from the Pinto-Coriat family, were hung on the walls.
Since 1969 the building and the Sephardi Museum (created in 1964) have belonged to the Spanish Ministry of Culture's State Museums network.
Between 1985 and 1992 the building was completely remodelled in order to adapt it to its present function as a museum: structural modifications were made; the stuccowork and the coffered ceiling were restored; excavations were made; and a new museum project was implemented.

The building

The building stands on a rectangular ground plan and has a hipped roof.

Façade of the Synagogue, from a drawing by F. Palomares, 1752.

Facing page: Synagogue of El Tránsito. View of the interior.

View of the east wall.

Photometric elevation of the stuccowork on the hekhal front. (I.C.R.B.C.)

The walls are of brick and masonry and have pointed arches in their upper part. The great prayer room is also rectangular. The roof, a pine eight-sided truss with double ties, is one of the finest examples of mediaeval Hispanic Muslim carpentry. Although some of its original colour is lost, greens, blues, reds, oranges, whites and blacks and some Arabic inscriptions are still visible.

Particularly outstanding is the stuccowork decoration on all the walls. This takes the form of ornamental and inscriptive bands which culminate in the east wall, where the ***hekhal*** – a special cabinet (***Aron Kodesh***) containing the Scrolls of the Law (***Sefarim***) – is situated. This is further testimony to the skill of

The coffered ceiling in the prayer room with its painted decoration.

the Mudéjar builders who gave form to a multitude of stuccowork stems, fruits, flowers, geometric designs, heraldic themes, columns, capitals and Hebrew inscriptions in different shades of green, blue, black and white (some of which were lost due to insufficiently supervised restoration work).
The arched windows contain pointed arches with latticework, producing an effect of carefully filtered light which would have combined with the light of the oil lamps described in one of the inscriptions.
With an entrance of its own, the women's gallery runs almost the whole length of the south wall and occupies the first floor above the present vestibule. Its five large openings overlook the interior of the synagogue, which would have allowed the women to follow the service while remaining apart from it. All around the upper section of the walls in this room (as in the rest of the building) there are vestiges of

Detail of the east wall.

Stuccowork on the hekhal front. Detail.

decorated stuccowork and bands with Hebrew inscriptions. Here stars and Kufic inscriptions alternate with unadorned ovals.
One feature of this synagogue which makes it a truly unique building are the **inscriptions.** These are typical of the Mudéjar art of the 13th-15th centuries. The Hebrew inscriptions can be divided into two main groups: **historical** and **biblical.**
In turn, the **historical** inscriptions can be subdivided into:

a) those which provide information on the synagogue's furnishings and outbuildings: the *bimah*, or *tevah* or platform, the Scrolls of the Law, crowns, plates, lamps, and the *beth hamidrash* or school where religious study took place.
b) those praising Samuel Halevi and King Peter, who authorized the synagogue's construction and is referred to as the "great eagle with huge wings".

The **biblical** inscriptions serve as an ornamental frame to the east wall and to the decorative garlands with vegetal motifs and latticework on the side and west walls of the Synagogue. They also adorn the women's gallery. The passages are taken from the books of Psalms, Chronicles, Kings and Exodus.
The Arabic inscriptions are repeated throughout the synagogue and serve as ornamentation.

Detail of the windows in the central hall.

THE SEPHARDI MUSEUM

ROOM I

Traditions of the Jewish people and their origins

The Jews in the ancient west

The ancient religious and cultural traditions of the Jews in their place of origin, the old Near East, are contained in the group of writings known by Jews as the *Tanach* (whose consonants correspond to the initial consonants of *Torah*, *Nebiim* and *Ketubim* = "the Law, the Prophets and the Scriptures") and which makes up part of the Old Testament in the Christian Bible. These religious traditions are interwoven in the Bible with events in the lives of the ancestors of the Jewish people, thus making up a religious history whose final version was drafted in the period of exile in the Neo-Babylonian Empire and during the return to and subsequent settlement in Palestine during the Persian and Hellenistic periods (6th-2nd centuries B.C.). They are not historical writings in the current sense of the term, but rather a "religious history" which attempts to explain the vicissitudes of the Jewish people, above all during the difficult times of exile and the return to and restoration of the Jewish institutions in Palestine. Thus any texts, maps or other references to the history of the ancient East used in this museum to illustrate the origins of the various Jewish traditions and institutions are merely to place these within the geographical and historical context of the ancient Near East where, according to the Bible, the Jewish religious and cultural traditions that live on in the Sephardic culture originated.

1. Patriarchal Traditions

The patriarchal traditions, in which the ancestors of the Jewish people are referred to as semi-nomads

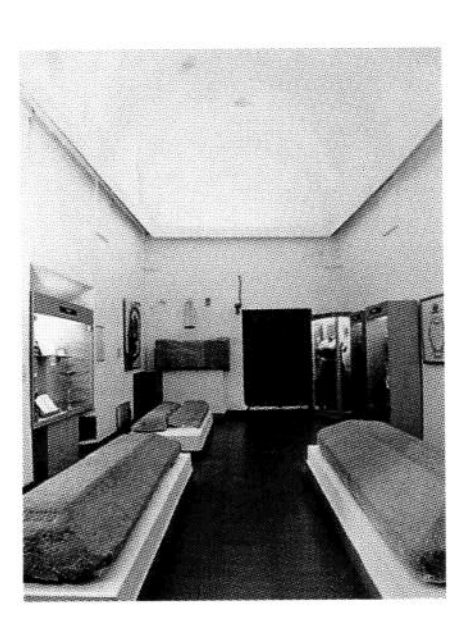

View of the Museum rooms in the 1980s.

Near East cabinet.

Map of the Near East.

outside Canaan, are to be found in the first half of the 2nd millennium B.C. From this period the museum possesses a number of **ceramic** (bowls, flagons) and **metal** objects (a bronze adze, a two-eyed axe).

Archaeological exhibits illustrating the geographical and historical background. On temporary loan from the Israel Antiquity Authority (Israel).

2. Traditions of the Exodus and settlement in Canaan. Tribal organisation. The Canaanite period

Traditionally, the Bible stories situate the Exodus in the first half of the 13th century B.C., during the reign of Ramses II. Although no historical texts exist confirming that the Israelites were actually present in Egypt and that they departed and conquered Canaan, a group – from which the Israelite tribes later formed – would seem to have appeared in the 13th-12th centuries B.C. From this period the museum possesses a number of **ceramic** items (jugs, figurines, a *bilbil*) and **metal** objects (an axe and a bronze figurine) and two soapstone scarabs.

3. The formation of a state. The United Kingdom and its division

Pressure from the technologically and culturally more highly developed Philistines posed a threat to the Israelites' survival. As an answer to this challenge, a monarchic system was established shortly before the year 1000 B.C. Under King David ancient Israel was to see its capital founded in Jerusalem for the first time. During the reign of Solomon large-scale constructions were built, the most famous being the Temple of Jerusalem – subsequently idealised as the centre of all future Jewish religious and civic life. After Solomon, the kingdom became divided into North and South and suffered a number of vicissitudes before finally being destroyed. From this period the museum possesses a number of **ceramic** (perfume holders, zoomorphic vessels) and **metal** objects (bronze bracelets).

4. Fall of the Kingdoms and exile

The resurgence of the Neo-Assyrian Empire brought disaster to the Northern kingdom and the capital fell to Sargon II in 722 B.C. As a result of various deportations imposed upon them, the Jewish people lost their identity. In the south, the kingdom of Judah survived as a vassal state first of the Assyrians and later of the Neo-Babylonians, until Nebuchadnezzar destroyed Jerusalem in 587 B.C. and removed the ruling class to Babylon. Part of the population sought refuge in Egypt. This was the germ of the later dispersions. Subsequent historical data on the exiles comes from the Persian period and later. From this time the most important item exhibited in the museum is, without any doubt, a pottery **ostracon** bearing a list of names. Next to it are other **ceramic** (figurines, lamps, pots, pitchers and part of a stamped handle) and **metal** items (a fibula and a bronze amulet).

5. The Diaspora in Persian and Hellenistic times

Having conquered Babylonia in 539 B.C., Cyrus issued an edict permitting the return of exiles. Around 520 B.C., the temple was rebuilt and the Jewish community re-formed in Judaea, which once more became the centre of "Judaism" and retained close links with the groups of Jews in Babylonia and Egypt. In Palestine the Jewish communities managed to avoid assimilation by Hellenism.

From the time of the Diaspora, the museum possesses **ceramic** items from the Persian period (stamped handles, a lamp, unguentaria, and a bowl) and **metal** objects (dishes and bracelets).

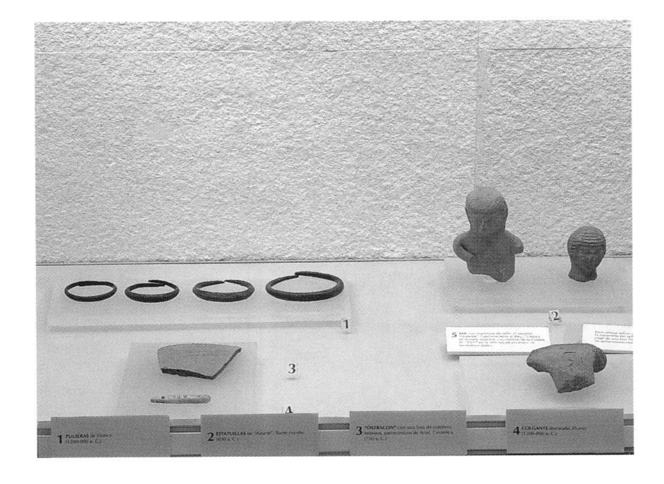

Archaeological exhibits illustrating the geographical and historical background. On temporary loan from the Israel Antiquity Authority (Israel).

6. UNDER THE ROMAN EMPIRE. THE JUDAEO-ROMAN WARS.

The expansion of Rome in the East reached Palestine under Pompey. The time of greatest splendour for the Jews came in the reign of Herod the Great (34 B.C.), who rebuilt the Temple of Jerusalem. Hopes of a new Messiah and restoration encouraged by sects such as the Zealots gave rise to revolts against Rome. The first such revolt was crushed by Vespasian and Titus and ended with the destruction of the Temple (70 A.D.); the leader of the second, when Hadrian was emperor, was Bar Kokhba, who fiercely resisted the Roman legions. Jerusalem fell in 134 A.D., leading to the dispersion of the Jewish people.

From this period the museum possesses a number of **ceramic** (candle holders, pots, an aryballos and an unguentarium) and **stone** items (a measuring vessel and a magnificent ossuary) and various bronze and silver **coins** dating from the 1st century B.C. to the 2nd century A.D.

Ossuary 1st Century A.D. Jerusalem, Kidron Valley, tomb no. 5.

Two six-petalled rosettes flanking a stylised tree. Vestiges of red paint. On the side, an inscription carved in Hebrew characters: *Shalun Bat Li'ezer*. Ossuaries were made from limestone blocks cut into rectangular boxes with four small supports or "feet". The lid, also of stone, could be smooth, curved or pediment-like. Sometimes the name of the deceased was incised in Hebrew on the ossuary by members of his/her family. The bones of the dead were placed in individual ossuaries which were then inserted into the niches of tombs dug in the rock. These tombs consisted of a chamber with several separate niches, which enabled whole families to be interred in the same grave.*

Archaeological exhibits illustrating the geographical and historical background. On temporary loan from the Israel Antiquity Authority (Israel).

Cabinet containing Judaica.

The synagogue in antiquity

The synagogue was different from the Temple in that the latter was unique and could only be situated in Jerusalem; it had no priests, nor were sacrifices made there. The synagogue can be built anywhere, in small or large cities alike, within or without the walls, in the Diaspora or in Israel. It has always adapted to the buildings around it and to the art styles predominant in each age. Wherever there have been ten Jewish men there has been a synagogue. When Jerusalem fell to the Romans in 70 A.D. and the Second Temple was destroyed, the **synagogue** became Judaism's most important institution.
The establishment of the synagogue as a place dedicated primarily to community worship and particularly to the teaching and reading of the *Torah* is attributed to the period of the Babylonian exile, after the destruction of the Temple of Solomon.

Judaism as a way of life

Throughout history, religion has been the most important aspect of life for Jews. It is the link between different groups and the driving force of day-to-day life, customs and celebrations. Judaism is based on the *Torah* (the Law, Pentateuch, the first five books of the Bible), the *Mishnah* (2nd century A.D.) and the *Talmud* (6th century A.D.), and rabbis have always taught the regulations prescribed in them to their communities. The synagogue is the institution which brings all this knowledge to life.
From the moment the Jewish male is circumcised on the eighth day after birth, he officially becomes a member of the community. In his

** All the archaeological items used to illustrate the geographical and historical framework in which the traditions that inspire the Jewish people take place are on temporary loan from the Israel Antiquity Authority (Israel).*

work *Kuzari*, the 11th-century Spanish poet Jehuda ha-Levi wrote that the Jew views the liturgical year as a period in which each moment has an important point.
All the hours of the day are oriented to the three times of prayer that take place in the synagogue:
In the week, on Saturday (Sabbath)

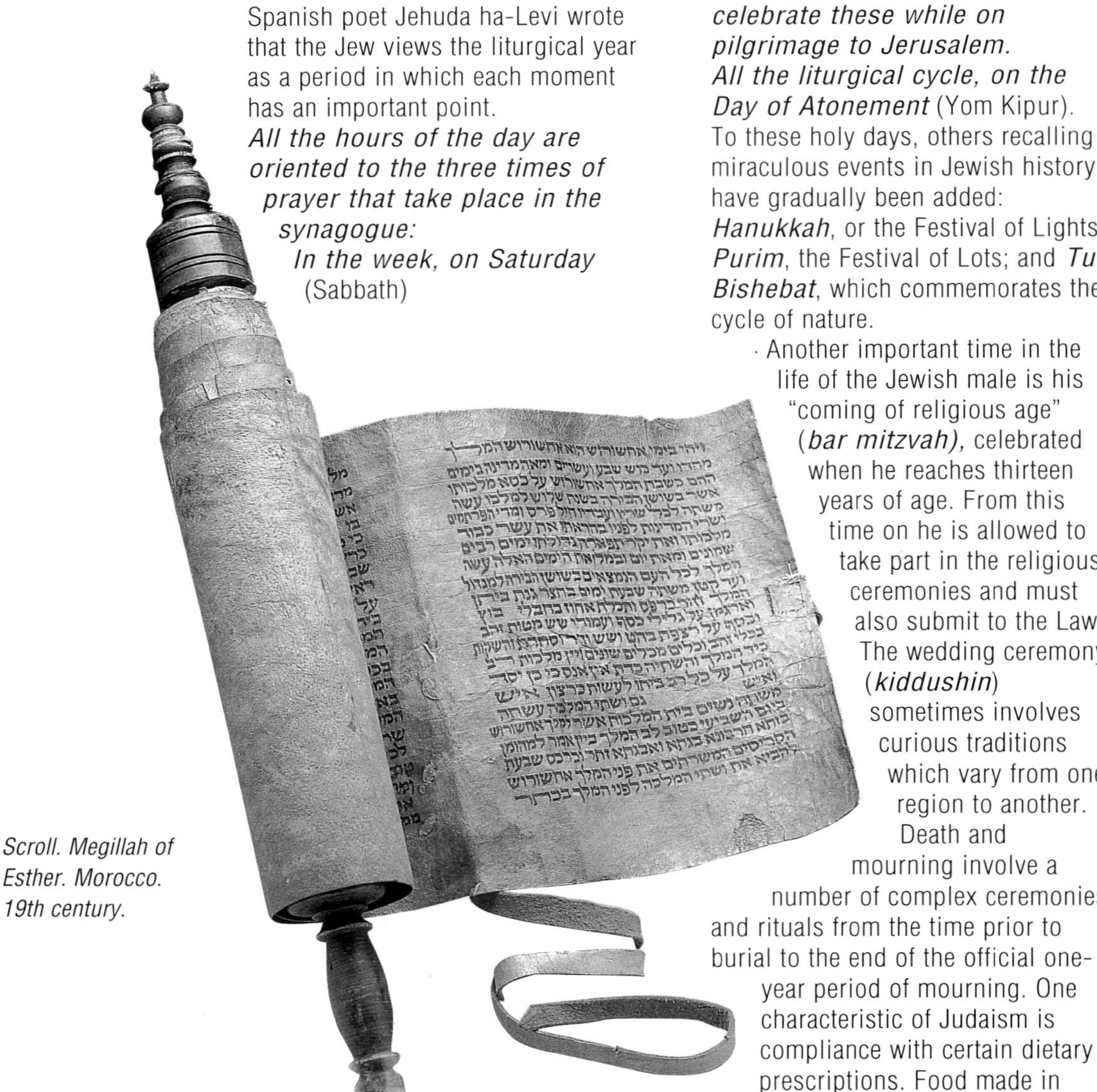

Scroll. Megillah of Esther. Morocco. 19th century.

In the month, on the day of the new moon (Yom ha-Hodesh)
In the times of the year of the three festivals of pilgrimage (*Shalosh ha-Regalim*), *for in Antiquity the custom was to celebrate these while on pilgrimage to Jerusalem.*
All the liturgical cycle, on the Day of Atonement (Yom Kipur).
To these holy days, others recalling miraculous events in Jewish history have gradually been added: *Hanukkah*, or the Festival of Lights; *Purim*, the Festival of Lots; and *Tu Bishebat*, which commemorates the cycle of nature.

Another important time in the life of the Jewish male is his "coming of religious age" *(bar mitzvah),* celebrated when he reaches thirteen years of age. From this time on he is allowed to take part in the religious ceremonies and must also submit to the Law. The wedding ceremony (*kiddushin*) sometimes involves curious traditions which vary from one region to another. Death and mourning involve a number of complex ceremonies and rituals from the time prior to burial to the end of the official one-year period of mourning. One characteristic of Judaism is compliance with certain dietary prescriptions. Food made in accordance with these is known as *kosher*, a term which covers not only the food itself but also its preparation.

The Torah

The *Torah* or Law is made up of the five books of the Pentateuch. According to the *Mishnah* or oral Law, Moses received the *Torah* from God on Mount Sinai, passed it on to Joshua, who in turn gave it to the elders and prophets, who brought it to the members of the Great Assembly.
There is not one superfluous word in the *Torah*, nor one letter without its special meaning. Study of the Torah is regarded as synonymous with communication with God and not as an intellectual exercise. The reading of the *Torah* is part of synagogue worship and takes place at least four times a week: on Saturdays, during the morning and evening services, and on Monday and Thursday mornings. The *Torah* is also read on the mornings of days when there is a new moon, on days of fasting, and at the *Hanukkah*, *Purim* and *Yom Kippur* festivals. At the *Simhath Torah* festival celebrated at the end of the Feast of Tabernacles (*Sukkot*), it is carried in procession. For this, the synagogue cabinet is opened and the *Torah* carried to the *tevah* or pulpit, which stands in the centre of the synagogue. As it passes, the members of the congregation kiss it or touch it with their *talliths*, which they then raise to their lips. In Sephardic communities the scroll is raised before the congregation after its mantle and adornments have been removed and before the reading begins.
The text of the *Torah* has no punctuation or accents, so that reading properly with the correct intonation requires study.
The material the text is written on and the way in which it is prepared, the inks and type of pen, and the writing of the characters must all fulfil a number of requirements laid down in the *Talmud*.

The Torah.

Amulet.

Reverence for the *Torah* scroll is expressed through the position it occupies in the synagogue and the ornamentation it bears. The *Torah* is like a queen and as such is honoured and arrayed. Thus it is covered with rich mantles of embroidered velvet and is crowned. To facilitate the reading of the *Torah* the scroll is rolled around two guides or spindles (*es ha-hayyim*) whose bottom end is shaped like a ball and on which it is rested. The top end, which is pointed, is fitted with silver adornments known as *rimmonim* or *tappuhim* whose shape depends on the place of origin. Each is decorated with small bells in imitation of those worn on the robe of the High Priest in the Temple of Solomon. It is also embellished with "breastplates" or necklaces hung with silver plates and sometimes inlaid with semi-precious stones. These bear the names of the main Jewish holy days and are sometimes inscribed with the commandments of Moses.

So that the sacred text will not be tainted through contact with the hand, a pointer known as a *yad* or *moreh* is used to follow it. This ends in the shape of a hand with an extended index finger which sometimes has a ring with a precious stone on it. This pointer is almost always made of either solid or hollow silver. Some are attached to the *Torah* scroll with a chain to ensure that they are not lost.

When a scroll deteriorates through use, it is no longer used in the religious service and, like all religious manuscripts, is buried. The "cemetery of manuscripts" is known as the *genizah*, and the most famous is in Cairo.

West side of the prayer room.

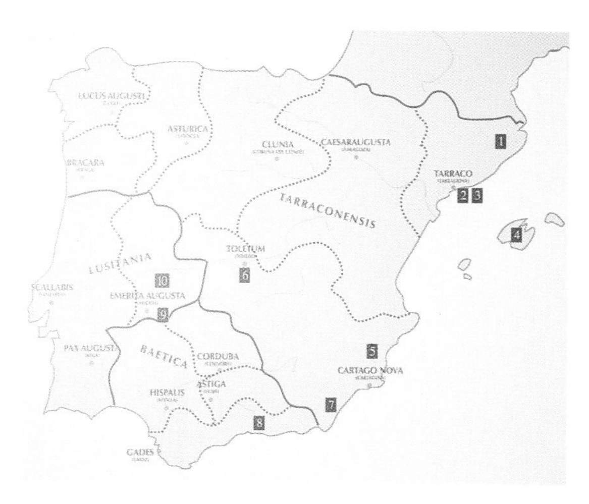

Left, "The Jews in Hispania". 2nd century B.C.- 5th century A.D.

Right, map of the Roman period.

Another object connected with the *Torah* is the box used by the Jews of Central Europe and the Yemenites for keeping the scrolls in. The curtains covering the place where the scrolls are kept and the strips of material which bind them are made from the clothing of newborn male children. These strips are offered to the synagogue so that those on whose behalf they are donated will later fulfil their obligations as Jews. Furthermore, carpets or tapestries are placed in front of the *tevah*, where the reading takes place.

ROOM II

THE JEWS IN ROMAN AND VISIGOTHIC TIMES

Writers of Roman times, such as Strabo, Juvenal, Tacitus, and above all Flavius Josephus (an extremely useful source on the Jewish world and its wars with the Romans), make no mention of the possible arrival of Jews in Hispania. However, while archaeological sources are not much more explicit, they do at least confirm the presence of Jews in Spain.

The first such source of confirmation dates from the 2nd century A.D. and takes the form of the funeral epigraph of a certain *Iustinus*, a native of Flavia Neapolis (now Shechem, Samaria) which was discovered in Mérida. Two more gravestones (dating from the 3rd century A.D. and now lost) were found in Villamesías (Cáceres) and Adra (Almería). From the 5th century A.D. comes the trilingual basin of Tarraco (Tarragona) and a fragment of a lamp decorated with a *menorah* (Toledo). The Jews reached Hispania during the early centuries of the empire in the wake of the troubles in Palestine after the wars in Judaea against Vespasian and Hadrian. Jews enjoyed a status similar to that of the rest of the citizens of the Roman empire, particularly after the Edict of Caracalla in 202 A.D. Having settled in Hispano-Roman towns, they made their contribution to the economic growth of the empire in the early centuries but were also to suffer the consequences of the troubles of the 3rd century A.D. and after. In accordance with the new situation, the Jews played their part in the economic recovery of certain towns, although others moved to the *villae*, where they were employed as paid workers on the large estates, as craftsmen trading with the estates, and, naturally, also as slaves. As is logical, certain important Jewish merchants became estate owners themselves, so that Jews held positions covering a broad social spectrum.

From the time of their arrival in Hispania, they were allowed to practise their religion freely thanks to the prevailing religious tolerance; consequently official, local and other Eastern religions coexisted within the same area.

It is clear that Christianity borrows from Judaism and this led to serious problems of proselytism between the two religions. This situation was reflected in the canons of the Council of Elvira (Granada, 306-312 A.D.) and recurred in subsequent Councils.

Nevertheless, more serious problems, such as the disintegration of the Roman world and the barbarian invasions, were of greater concern to the Hispano-Romans and the Jews. This is reflected in the most important record concerning the life of the Jewish communities of Hispania, a letter from Bishop Severus of Minorca (5th century A.D.). The most important archaeological remains from this period are the synagogue of Elche. Built in the 4th century A.D., it is the oldest known synagogue in Spain. It stands on a rectangular ground plan and its most important feature is a mosaic decorated with three or four bands of colour and Greek inscriptions referring to "The Archons and the Presbyters" and the "People's place of prayer".

Although archaeological remains attributable to the Jewish communities of the Visigothic era (6th-7th centuries) are also scarce, thanks to documentary evidence it

"The Jews in Visigothic Times". 6th-7th centuries A.D.

can be said that the ancient Jewish communities which settled in Hispania during the first centuries of the empire continued to exist and even to thrive.
Until Recared converted to Catholicism in 589, the Visigothic kings were Arians, but with their conversion to Christianity, the Jews became the most important religious minority in the country.
Through the policy dictated by the various councils, the Church, as an institution directly concerned with the problems of proselytism, began to attack Judaic practices in an attempt to force the Jewish communities to embrace Catholicism. Nevertheless, it seems that during the whole of the 6th century and the beginning of the 7th the Jewish communities had no great trouble in leading a normal life, and were completely integrated into the Hispanic Visigothic socio-economic environment which followed that of the late Roman period.
But the panorama was to change drastically between the middle and the end of the 7th century, for it is during this period that we can speak of persecution and even violence, leading to outbreaks of messianism which by generating instability within the realm led to an ever-worsening situation. Because of this, the arrival of Muslim troops in the Iberian peninsula came as a relief to the Jews and was welcomed by them.

The Synagogue of Elche, courtesy of the German Archaeological Institute.

THE SYNAGOGUE OF ELCHE (4TH CENTURY)

The synagogue of Elche was excavated in 1905 by Ibarra and Albertini. According to Ibarra it was "a perfect quadrilateral 10.9 metres long by 7.55 metres wide, the longer sides being oriented from east to west. On the east side were remains of a semi-circular apse one metre high. The rectangle could be distinguished perfectly as the floor

Gravestone of a Rabbi. Mérida (Badajoz). 7th-8th century A.D.

was covered with mosaic whose shape was clearly recognizable". The mosaic consists of three bands in four colours: black, white, red and bright yellow. One is on the north side, another in the centre and the third on the south side; one with three inscriptions in Greek is also in this area. As regards the purpose and age of the building there are two – opposing – theories.
Albertini believed it was a 4th-century **synagogue** which later became a Christian basilica.
Other authors, including Seimour, De Ricci, Reinach, Frey, and more recently Palol and García Iglesias, are of the same opinion.
Ibarra, on the other hand, believed it was a Christian **basilica** dating from the 5th or 6th century. His view, which is shared by Puig Cadafech and Lampérez, was published in *Historia de España* (edited by Menéndez Pidal) and in *Ars Hispaniae*. Professor Schlunk has recently expressed the same opinion, but believes the building dates from the 4th or 5th century.
Although the evidence is still not completely conclusive, we are inclined to believe the building is a synagogue, in which case it is the oldest in Spain, although it may have been used as a basilica at a later date. Furthermore, a number of other basilicas with mosaics studied by Palol in Mallorca could have undergone the same transformation as that in Elche.
The inscriptions in Greek refer to the "Archons and the Presbyters", i.e. to the Elders, and the "People's place of prayer", which is more in keeping with the building's use as a synagogue than as a basilica. It is known that the items of furniture used in the synagogues of that time included chairs for the elders, who sat, in accordance with the old tradition, facing the congregation with their backs to the cabinets containing the Scroll of the Law.
Furthermore, according to Dimas Fernández-Galiano, the mosaic clearly dates from the 4th century A.D. as it is similar to others found in late-Roman *villae* in the same area and coincides with those at other sites. Photograph, courtesy of the German Institute of Archaeology.

Funeral epigraph of Iustinus, a native of Flavia Neapolis (now Shechem, Samaria) discovered in Emérita Augusta (now Mérida) in the 2nd century A.D. Copy. Museo de Arte Romano, Mérida.

Fragment from Lucerna, decorated with a menorah. toledo. 5th century A.D.

Gravestone. Mérida (Badajoz). 7th century A.D.

This room contains the museum's most valuable item, the **Trilingual Basin.** 5th century A.D. (Tarraco, now Tarragona).
A rectangular, white marble basin with a drain hole at the centre, it has been described as a basin for ablutions in the synagogue (subsequently used for other purposes). The front is decorated with a seven-branched candelabrum (*menorah*) flanked by two peacocks, the one on the right eating fruit from a tree, the one on the left pecking at a serpent. There is a two-line legend in irregular Hebrew characters on one of the peacocks: *Peace unto Israel and unto us and unto our children, Amen.*
The basin bears two more inscriptions (also in irregular characters) one in Latin – *Pax Fides* – the other in Greek – *FAH.*

Trilingual basin (Tarraco, now Tarragona).

Menorah engraved on sandstone. Eremitorio. Ercávica (Cuenca). 6th or 7th century A.D.

Funeral brick decorated with a menorah. Acinipo. Malaga. 4th century A.D.

Room II,

Room II,

THE JEWS IN AL-ANDALUS

In 711, Muslim troops led by Tariq ibn Ziyad crossed the Strait of Gibraltar and began to penetrate the Iberian Peninsula (bringing the Visigothic kingdom to an end a few years later). After more than a century of persecution, the Jews welcomed the Muslims as liberators and aided them in their campaigns. Although obliged to pay special taxes, they enjoyed religious freedom and a relative state of well-being.
During the first centuries of Muslim domination the Jewish communities flourished and were allowed to administer themselves autonomously. The Umayyad emirate of Córdoba (756-952) consolidated Islamic power and favoured the growth of Jewish communities such as those in the cities of Mérida and Córdoba. During the caliphate of Abd ar-Rahman III (912-961) the unity and splendour of the State was reinforced, and Córdoba became the main centre of culture and the arts. The Jews of Córdoba and those who came across the sea from other Hispanic cities in North Africa and the East, enjoyed a time of great cultural splendour prompted by Abu Yusuf Hisdai ibn Shaprut.
At the beginning of the 11th century, the caliphate of Córdoba collapsed, and after several turbulent years the ***taifa*** kingdoms began to form. Although these were small, weak states rife with conflict and rivalry, some managed to attain short-lived greatness. In the Zirid kingdom of Granada, under the dominion of the Berbers, Samuel ibn Nagrela (993-1056) rose to a high position at court.
By this time Lucena, Seville, Saragossa and Toledo, among other cities, had large Jewish communities, some of

whose members were prominent writers, men of science and royal physicians and counsellors. Under pressure from the Christians, who managed to conquer Toledo in 1085, the rulers of various *taifas* asked the Almoravid sultan Yusuf ibn Tashufin for help. In the last decade of the century, the Almoravids conquered these kingdoms one by one. With the Almoravids the position of the Jews became extremely delicate and a considerable number fled to the less culturally developed Castile. Thus, in Granada, for example, few Jews remained. Some years later, the moral and military decline of the Almoravids, internal revolts and the Christian advances facilitated the arrival of the Almohads, who from 1147 conquered the cities in Al-Andalus which had previously belonged to the Almoravid kingdom.

The Almohad troops brought the splendour of Jewish culture in Al-Andalus to an end and the Jewish communities suffered seriously as a consequence. Among those faced with the choice of conversion to Islam or exile were the philologist Joseph Kimhi, the master translator Judah ibn Tibbon (who fled to Lunel and took the knowledge of the Jews of Al-Andalus to the European Jewish communities), and Moses ben Maimon (Maimonides), who fled to Egypt and there worked as a physician and philosopher.

The Almohad advance was halted at the battle of Navas de Tolosa in 1212. With their kingdom further weakened by internal strife, they were no longer able to face the Christian kings, who continued to advance on their frontiers. Ferdinand III took Córdoba in 1236 and Seville in 1248,
granting Jews a number of privileges and employing them in his administration. The wealthy and cultivated Jews in these communities aided the Christian kings in the task of resettling the abandoned territories. Under Christian rule the Jews of Al-Andalus enjoyed a period of peace and relative tolerance until the end of the 14th century, when a strong wave of anti-Jewish feeling instigated by the

Gravestone from Lucerna. White limestone. The Hebrew inscription on one of the sides appears to be an incomplete draft for that on the other side. Due to the archaic appearance of the characters, it probably dates from the 11th century.

Seville. Cathedral. Keys. 13th century.

Archdeacon of Écija, Ferrand Martínez, led in 1391 to attacks first on the Al-Andalusian communities and subsequently on those of the two Castiles and Aragon. As a result, Jews were forced either to be baptized as Christians or die for their religion, synagogues were converted into churches, and Jewish neighbourhoods were repopulated by Christians.
Throughout the 15th century some communities, including those in Córdoba and Seville, began slowly to recover from the disasters, but they were never again to reach the numbers or importance of previous centuries.
Coexistence between the converts (who continued to practise Judaism in clandestinity) and the old Christians led to a number of problems. In 1481 the Inquisition was established in the states belonging to Castile, and in 1483 a decree of expulsion was dictated against the Jews of Al-Andalus.
During various periods of persecution, a number of Jews sought refuge in the Nasrid kingdom of Granada (which survived until 1492). There the policy of the Muslim kings was one of tolerance, and asylum was granted to Jews fleeing from the Christian kingdoms. During the 15th century the Jews in this area numbered approximately one thousand, a small figure when compared with the number of Muslims.
Before capitulating to the Christian Monarchs, the last king of Granada requested that the Jews be treated in the same way as other groups – to be allowed judicial autonomy, freedom to practise their religion and permission to emigrate – but no heed was paid to him. Shortly after the fall of Granada, the expulsion edict of 1492 put an end to what remained of Jewish life in this region.
In Al-Andalus the majority of Jews had been merchants who exported leather goods, textiles and Al-Andalusian goldwork. Jews had also dominated the slave trade, on their frequent long journeys halting in the Jewish quarters of the towns they passed through.
Although some had been tax collectors

and bankers, such professions were not typical of Jews, for others had been tradesmen – carpenters, goldsmiths, silk weavers, etc. Jews were also tanners and dyers and there is evidence of the existence of Jewish shoemakers in Saragossa. Due to their knowledge of languages, they also worked as translators and on many occasions as interpreters, some working on the translation of philosophical and scientific works into Hebrew and Latin. Jews also became well-known as physicians and were often called to court to serve the kings.
The cabinet contains **silver gilt keys.** They are copies whose originals may be seen in Seville Cathedral.
A key presented to Ferdinand III by the Jews on his conquest of Seville in 1248. The letters on the bit read: *Dios abrirá / rey entrará* ("God shall open, king shall enter"). Around the edge of the head is the Hebrew inscription: *El rey de reyes abrirá, el rey de toda la tierra entrará* ("The king of kings shall open, the king of all the earth shall enter"). On the four sides immediately below this are alternating depictions of galleys and ships. The bowtel below displays castles and lions from the royal shield.
The smaller key was presented by the Arabs of Seville also to Ferdinand III. Copy by F. Marmolejo, goldsmith of Seville.
Both keys donated by the "Friends of the Museum Association".

The synagogue of Córdoba

In Córdoba nothing more remains than a synagogue building which, due to its size, appears to be a small oratory or a private synagogue rather than a communal building. From the inscription on the east wall it is known to have been built in 1315 by Isaac Moheb. When the Jews were expelled, the building became a hospital for rabies patients and was dedicated to St. Quiteria. In 1588 it became the property of the city's shoemakers' guild (dedicated to Saints Crispin and Crispinian) and it was used for chapter meetings and the celebration of patron saints' days. During this time it was adapted to Christian worship with altarpieces, altars and images.

Detail of the Synagogue of Córdoba.

Furthermore, the stuccowork and inscriptions were painted over with whitewash to such an extent that experts on monumental buildings were completely unaware of their existence. Around the end of the 18th century, when the roof was found to be damaged, a vault was built – hiding the beautiful coffered ceiling – and the stuccowork in the upper part of the building was seriously damaged. In 1884, Mariano Párraga discovered the vegetal motif stuccowork and latticework hidden beneath the additions made by the Christians.

Built in the Mudéjar style, the synagogue appears to have had some connection with the "Moor of Toledo's Workshop", the synagogue of El Tránsito in Toledo, and that in Cuenca (now lost). The exterior displays nothing to suggest the splendour that lies within. Nor is the entrance to the building monumental, as there is no more than a small courtyard in front of it. Standing on an almost quadrilateral ground plan, it contains, like the El Tránsito, a women's gallery. The decorative motifs, tiling and tapestries in the lower part – assuming these

The courtyard containing the gravestones.

once existed – are now lost. However, what does remain gives a magnificent impression of the beauty of the interior. As corresponds to the area in which the Scrolls of the *Torah* were kept, the east wall is the most highly-adorned. As in the El Tránsito, this wall contains a niche in which the scrolls were kept. In addition to the classical Mudéjar ornamentation, both this wall and those that remain bear Hebrew inscriptions. Except for the inscription mentioned above (which is historical and contains information on the construction of the building), these contain passages from the books of Psalms (primarily), Proverbs and Isaiah. The Hebrew characters are noteworthy for their regularity and their still intact colour. The Kufic inscriptions repeat the legend: *To Allah all dominion and power.*

NORTH COURTYARD

Mediaeval Spanish gravestones

In this courtyard, which is set out like a cemetery, some of the gravestones belonging to the museum (and coming from various parts of Spain) are on display.
They are made of a variety of materials, although it was customary in each area to draw on the material that was most readily available locally. Those of marble (the smallest in number), are commonly found in Old Castile, while those made of limestone and sandstone (easy materials to work with) are the most numerous, being commonly found in cemeteries in Gerona and Barcelona. In Toledo, the predominant material is granite, although the other materials mentioned above are also to be found and the museum even possesses one of baked clay.
The inscriptions on these gravestones are all very similar: they normally include the name of the deceased or that of his/her father, in the case of a woman that of her husband or father, and sometimes the date (day, month, year) and cause of death. They also include liturgical eulogies and formulae containing passages from the Bible, for example Daniel 12: 13: "For thou shalt rest, and stand in thy lot at the end of the days". Another expression often seen is: "Rest in Eden". At the end of the legend "Amen" or "So be it" is often found.
In many cases these inscriptions are like a funeral song honouring the deceased by extolling his/her virtues. Contrary to the custom in other cultures, drawings or symbols linked to the epigraph are rarely found on these gravestones.
The museum possesses around two hundred gravestones and although this is not a large number, there are enough to provide information on some of the most prominent families: Abulafia, Ibn Susan, Aser, Alfakhar, Ibn Nahmías...
Where categorising these graves into specific types is concerned, some experts have ventured to give opinions, but no particular model in which to include them can be established.
The most important items came from the Jewish cemeteries of Toledo, Barcelona (Montjuich), Gerona, León, Palencia, La Palloza (Galicia), Béjar (Salamanca), and Andalusia. The museum possesses a number of extremely important inscriptions. Furthermore there is a great deal of documentary information on

Detail of a gravestone in the north courtyard.

cemeteries (Judizmendi, for example) and other inscriptions that are now lost.
Poem by Moses Ibn Ezra
(On the wall of the North Courtyard)

They are old tombs, of ancient times,
in which men sleep the eternal sleep.
Within there is neither hatred nor envy,
nor the love or enmity of neighbours.
When I see them my mind is not able
to distinguish between slaves and lords.

Granite gravestone.
This comes from Béjar (Salamanca). The Hebrew inscription follows the shape of the stone. The characters are extremely original as they seem to have been carved with a double outline. They are large in size – 17 cm. This one is dedicated to *Doña Fadueña* and is from the late-13th or early-14th century. The inscription begins in the top right-hand corner.

Lady Fadueña
rest in glory,
glorious princess
within.

A gravestone in the north courtyard.

The **white marble gravestone** is in three pieces. Its Hebrew inscription is set out in eight and a half lines. It recalls R. Salomón, son of Abraham ben Yais. The stone bearing the inscription is a Roman cippus. The upper part of the inscription is in very bad condition. It comes from the Jewish cemetery close to the Campo del Zebrero or Ventilla in Seville.
Before it was recovered, it had been used for other purposes in Seville Cathedral. It is dated 1345.

Who sees in conspiracy those who...?
against me
opened the eye of ...my fate;
because of ....on my eyelids
I...keenly? ...my footwear.
Who crushes (tramples or vexes) a man...
amid his net drew my foot.
A witness be these stones, a witness this stele, as a sign and memory. It is written that / here was buried a museum of every precious object concerning the Law and the Testimony, and in the science of / the stars he spoke marvels, and with him was hidden a book of Medicine. Tree of knowledge, / an expert physician, pious, upright and truthful: R. Salomón, son of R. Abraham ben Yais – may he rest in glory – was reunited with his people, walking in his integrity, in the month of Sivan in the year five / thousand one hundred and five (1345) of the Creation.

Finally, the **granite gravestone**, which is coffin-shaped, was used as a surface for washing. It bears an inscription to Mrs. Sitbona, daughter of R. Petahya, son of Sahwán, and wife of R. Meir ha-Leví bar Isaac ha-Leví. Dated 1349, it comes from the Convent of Santo Domingo el Real in Toledo.

Follow, follow the road / that to God's house rises / and remove thy sandals; move aside in the field of first fruit and its path; for the road to holiness should be the name / of the estate of happiness where lies the grave of a great and noble lady, a great woman. / Thus was Mrs. Sitbona, daughter of that man, one of the lords of the country, / who stood his ground for the sake of the people of Yahweh, / R. Yehudá ben Peta ya – may he rest in glory, – son of Sahwán; wife of the great man / height of happiness and a sentinel – / R. Meir ha Leví bar Isaac ha-Leví – may he rest in glory! – / Died a victim of the plague during the month of Sivan, in the year 1349. Oh princess!, happy thou and thy fortune, / for thou hast multiplied thy charity and thy justice / and thou hast accumulated provisions for thy journey, / and through the rectitude of thy actions and through the honour of thy kindness and thy works. Take ample space in thy garden of delights, / under the wings of thy Rock, for He is thy Lord / and at the end of all days He shall resurrect thee to pay thee thy reward for thy work, for there is hope for thy future. At the resurrection of His devout dead / He shall say unto thee: Be not afflicted, shake off the dust, arise, be thou seated.

View of Room III.

ROOM III

THE JEWS IN THE CHRISTIAN KINGDOMS (13TH–15TH CENTURIES)

Exterior of Room III, with a model of Toledo.

With the advances of the Christian "Reconquest" and the arrival of the Almoravids and Almohads in the late-11th and early–12th centuries, most Jews became subjects of the Christian kingdoms, where, considered as Crown property, they enjoyed a special legal status and successive monarchs were able to count on their cooperation in repopulating the occupied territories. Jews were experts in administration, possessed great scientific knowledge and spoke Arabic, and so came to hold public positions, some as important as translators and interpreters, and even as Royal Treasurers for the kings of Castile and Aragon. The kings' physicians and counsellors were often also Jews.

By the middle of the 13th century the whole of the Peninsula except for the kingdom of Granada was Christian. This period – during the reigns of Alfonso X and Jaime I – was the greatest in the history of the Jews of Castile and Aragon. One of the most flourishing Jewish communities was that of Toledo, whose members included great rabbis, writers, financiers and statesmen such as the Ben–Sosáns and the Ben–Sadocs. Indeed, at this time there were over five hundred Jewish quarters and communities in the Peninsula. Examples of such communities in Castile are those of Burgos, Cuenca, León and Palencia. In the kingdom of Aragon this period saw the appearance of the great figures of Judaism such as Nahmanides of Gerona and Solomon ben Adret of Barcelona. The Montjuich cemetery is an example of the strength of these communities. In Navarre the situation was similar, with Tudela the main centre of Jewish life and culture.

Between the end of the 13th century and 1492, coexistence between Jews and Christians, once so good, gradually

deteriorated. In 1391 the anti–Jewish sermons of the archdeacon of Seville, Ferrán Martínez, led to attacks on and the destruction of a number of Jewish quarters. The sermons of Vincent Ferrer in 1414 led to massive conversions and the disappearance or decline of many other communities, and finally, in 1492, the Catholic Kings signed the Edict of Expulsion of the Jews. Most of those expelled went to Portugal and from there to North Africa. Others went to Italy, France and Holland, and in the course of the 16th century spread along both shores of the Mediterranean. Many Sephardic Jews settled in the Ottoman Empire.

As the Jewish quarters of Toledo, León, Palencia, Barcelona, Gerona, Segovia, Teruel, Salamanca, Soria, Cuenca and Valencia, among many others, had flourished both economically and culturally, archaeological remains are both interesting and numerous. These take the form of funeral epigraphs and a huge number of literary and scientific works and illuminated manuscripts. However, virtually no liturgical objects or items of everyday use have survived, although those of the Jews would presumably have been no different from those of the Christians or Mudéjars.

The Spanish Jews made an important contribution to the **economies** of the peninsular kingdoms. Many became landowners and held high public positions as diplomats, ministers, counsellors, senior Treasury officials, administrators of Crown property, and other legal posts. Jews were also concessionaires of royal mills and salt mines.

Jewish **society** was divided into three social classes. One group was formed by Jews who held senior posts in state administration and became courtiers, diplomats (due to their knowledge of languages), tax collectors and financiers. A second group was made up of rich traders, merchants, apothecaries and rag dealers; all of these lent out large sums of money which yielded high profits (hard to control, although an attempt was made through usury laws) which they then reinvested in real estate. The last group was made up of craftsmen, shopkeepers, tailors, shoemakers, milliners, clog makers, dyers,

Left, limestone bilingual capital. Toledo. 12th-13th century.

Above, details of fragments of stuccowork decoration from the Synagogue of Cuenca. Copies.

Funerary steles with Hebrew inscriptions. Monzón de Campos.

tanners, mail makers, bookbinders, goldsmiths, silversmiths and the occasional metal beater. A considerable number of these were also moneylenders.
Jews excelled in astronomy, medicine and surgery, some becoming physicians and surgeons to the kings. They not only treated their patients for the diseases and illnesses typical of the times but also for injuries due to falls from horses, broken bones, wounds of all kinds (sometimes caused by weapons), sores, ulcers, abbesses, fistulas, etc. The financial situation of these Jews varied from comfortable (in which case they lent money) to having just enough to live on. There were also a number of intellectuals, rabbis and scholars of the *Torah* or Jewish law; these were normally maintained by the community.
In their dress Jews were generally not distinguishable from their neighbours, although by law they were obliged to wear a badge in the form of a small red wheel or circle (*rodela*) to set them apart from non–Jews.
The homes of Jews reflected their owners' financial position and inventories have provided details on some of the items found in Jewish households.

Funerary stele with a Hebrew inscription. Marble. Puente Castro (León) 12th century.

Bilingual capital.

Coexistence between Jews and Christians

Apart from the confrontations arising out of mutual distrust and religious differences at certain, specific times, relations between Christians, Moors, Jews and converts were often friendly. For example, members of one community often visited others on their respective feast days and celebrations and took an interest in their liturgies and customs; furthermore, these group often had dealings with each other in matters connected with finance, trade, and services. In areas with small populations or on estates under a lord, social contact between the three religious groups was more frequent and Christians would often be invited to Jewish or Moorish weddings. When the demands of the local

lord were abusive, the three groups sometimes supported one another. Feast days and celebrations brought together not only members of one community but also those of neighbouring communities. Birth and death were causes for general happiness or mourning. The first served as a good excuse to visit and make gifts to the newborn child and its mother. However, at a certain time such coexistence shattered and gave rise to a climate of violence against Jews which increased in vehemence throughout the 15th century. The Catholic Kings established the Inquisition to serve the crown in consolidating political and religious unity within their realms and to put an end to the question of the false converts known as "crypto–Jews".

Indeed, the monarchs went so far as to say that converts could not become good Christians while Jews continued to live alongside them. Consequently in 1492 they decreed the expulsion from the kingdom of all Jews who would not convert to Christianity.
One of the main exhibits in this room is a limestone **bilingual capital** from Toledo (12th or 13th century). In Hebrew: "Blessed shalt thou be when thou comest in, and blessed shalt thou be when thou goest out" (Deut. 28:6). In Arabic: "Blessing and happiness, success and peace". Possible origin: a synagogue building in Toledo. Another important exhibit is a group of **three plates and two small spoons.** Made of silver, they are copies. The originals were found in

A plate. Burgos.

Copies of the three plates and two small spoons. Silver.

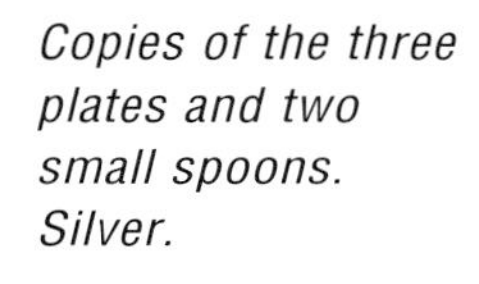

Oil on cardboard. Santa María la Blanca (Toledo). Ricardo Madrazo.

Watercolour. Interior of the main synagogue in Segovia before the fire of 1899. Ricardo Madrazo.

Briviesca (Burgos), at nos. 44–46 Calle de los Baños, in the old Jewish quarter, during the construction of a new building. A total of five plates, two small spoons, several hundred copper and silver coins from the reign of Peter I and fragments of pottery were found there. In 1988 excavations revealed part of the structure of a house (and a street) rased by a fire. The richness of the items suggests that they formed part of tableware used during the Feast of the Passover (*Pesah*). Original in the Museum of Burgos. Copy made by the Burgos goldsmith Maese Calvo e Hijos.
The museum also possesses a **Gravestone** with a Hebrew inscription. Marble. Puente Castro (León), 12th century. The inscription reads:
This is the grave of Mar H[iyya (?) son of] / Mar José ben 'Aziz the goldsmith, who died / at the age of sixty–five years, the first day / of the week, (Sunday), *on the fifteenth day of the month / of Kislev, in the year eight / hundred and sixty–one (1100 A.D.) in the reckoning of / the city of León. May the Saint, blessed be he! absolve him, / forgive his trespasses, expiate / his sins, have mercy on him, / keep him for his fate at the end of the days / and resurrect him to life in the future world.*
Another important item in this room is a

watercolour depicting the interior of the main synagogue in Segovia before the fire of 1899 (now the Church of Corpus Christi). Painted by Ricardo Madrazo (Madrid, 1852–1917), member of an illustrious family of painters (grandson of José Madrazo and son of Federico Madrazo). He was also the nephew of Mariano Fortuny. A pupil of his father's and Fortuny's, he is the least–known member of the family. Ricardo Madrazo painted what was once the interior of the main synagogue in Segovia, entitling his picture *Iglesia del Corpus Christi.* The painter's signature is in the bottom left–hand corner: *R. de M.* Below this is: *Iglesia del Corpus Cristi / Segovia, 1883.* A note written by the painter at the bottom of the picture reads: *Very similar to S. la Blanca) / in Toledo / between the columns* (sic) */ 5 aisles* (followed by a blank line). *An aisle with / three columns and another against the wall.* Written in red pencil in the top left–hand corner on the back of the picture is: *Ricardo Madrazo,* and below this: *Watercolour by my father Ricardo Madrazo. I bear witness: his son Mariano Madrazo* (undated). In the middle is the number 74 and written in a different hand in black pencil: *Atanea / pap* (paper) *canso* (thickness) / 7 cm. long / 1006 *reales* (sic).
Ricardo Madrazo's picture shows a view of the interior of the synagogue (which was converted into a church in 1910). With soft tones and skilfully applied brush–strokes he offered an intimist view of the building. Furthermore, he managed with rare proficiency to convey a sensation of loneliness and sadness in this beautiful building.
Donated by the "Friends of the Sephardi Museum of Toledo Association".

Hispanic–jewish Culture

It is indeed surprising when one opens the fan of Hispanic Hebrew culture, for we are instantly dazzled by its rich and varied intellectual and artistic panorama. Despite risk of oversimplification, who could forget the names of such men as Menahem ben Saruq of Tortosa or Dunash ben Labrat with their high standing, as early as the ***10th century,*** *in the field of philology, with their observations on the science of* ***comparative linguistics,*** *observations which placed them many centuries before their time? Nor can we disregard those who excelled in the brilliant artistic and intellectual life of the* Taifas, *such as Solomon ibn Gabirol (Avicebron to the Latin world), or Bahya ibn Pakuda at the court of the Tujibids and the Hudids of Saragossa, or Samuel ibn*

Silver earrings. Montjuich cemetery (Barcelona). 13th-14th century.

Toledo. Jewish quarter. Pottery. 14th century. On loan from J. Aguado (Toledo).

Nagrela, vizier to the Zirids of Granada, poet, philologist and ***Talmudist,*** *or the* ***poets and thinkers*** *of Lucena, such as Ishaq ben Gayyat, or of Barcelona, such as Ishaq ben Reuben Al–Bargeloni, or of Granada, such as Moses ibn Ezra, or of Tudela, such as Judah ha–Levi. And in the period after the turmoil caused by the invasion of the fanatical Almohads in the middle of the* ***12th century:*** *how can we not pronounce the names of Maimonides, Abraham ibn Ezra, Nahmanides, Solomon ben Adret? And finally, in a less dynamic period – from* ***the 13th to the 15th century*** *– how could be forget the* ***theological and philosophical*** *school of Hasdai Crescas and Joseph Albo in Aragon–Catalonia, the* ***scientific work*** *of Abraham Zacuto or the poetry of Solomon ben Meshullam de Pierà and of so many, many others?*

(This passage from Federico Pérez Castro's "España y los judíos españoles", published in *The Sephardi Heritage*, edited by Richard Barnett, 1971, is reproduced as a tribute to the curator and the man who inspired this Museum in the first years of its existence.)

Is there a sea between us
that prevents me from going to honour thee in death
and running with my heart pounding
to sit by thy grave?
In truth, if I did not do so
I would betray thy love as a brother
by thy grave, facing thee;
for thee my heart mourns,
as it doth for thy death.
I greet thee
and I hear not thy answer.
Thou comest not out to meet me
when I come to thy land.
Thou laughest not when I am near thee
nor do I laugh when I have thee at my side.
Thou canst not see my face,
nor I thine,
for Sheol is thy house
and the grave thy abode.
First–born of my father and my mother,
may peace be with thee henceforth.
May the spirit of God rest
on thy spirit and on thy soul.
I return to my land, thou remainest
a prisoner of the earth.
I sleep and awake
thou sleepest now forever.
Till the day of my passing
the fire of thy absence will burn
in my heart.

Samuel ibn Nagrela,
10th–11th century.

Ceramic bowl. 14th-15th century. Toledo.

HISPANIC–JEWISH ILLUMINATED MANUSCRIPTS

The embellishment of Hebrew biblical books, manuscripts, prayers and other writings became one of the most important ways in which the Jews of Spain expressed their devotion to the written word.
The most beautiful illuminated Bibles (Burgos, 13th century; Cervera, 14th century; Soria, 14th century; Toledo, 14th century and Lisbon, 15th century) and *Haggadoth* (Sarajevo, Kaufman, Golden) in the world were made in Spain by Catalan, Castilian, Aragonese and Mallorcan Jews.
As far as decorative elements – pages covered mainly with floral, geometric and minute motifs – are concerned, these illuminated manuscripts are very similar to the ones produced in the East. They also serve as a source of information on the life and customs of the Hispanic Jews, on the way they dressed, the interiors of their places of worship, etc.
The expulsions from Spain in 1492 and Navarre in 1497 caused the Jews to disperse throughout Europe and North Africa. The illuminated manuscripts they took with them subsequently influenced those produced in Italy, Turkey, Tunisia and Yemen.
The cabinet contains a **page from the *Damascus Keter.*** Parchment. Burgos, 13th century.
A Bible copied in Burgos in 1260 by Menahem bar Abraham ibn Malik, Hispanic Jewish Castilian School.

A page from the "Damascus Keter".

This page now forms part of the Museum's collection, thanks to the invaluable help of Manuel Ramos Armero (R.I.P.).

THE INQUISITION AND THE CONVERTS

The Inquisition was an ecclesiastic court whose function was to eradicate heresy.
It was established on 1st November 1478 through a bull issued by Pope Sixtus IV and came under the jurisdiction of the Catholic Kings. It

Seal of Pedro I. Obverse and verso (14th century).

existed for 453 years and was abolished on 15th July 1834 through a decree issued by the government of the Regent María Cristina.
The Catholic Kings established the Inquisition as a vehicle to serve the crown in consolidating political and religious unity within their realms and so put an end to the problem of the false converts known as "crypto–Jews". Indeed, the monarchs went so far as to say that the converts could not become good Christians while Jews continued to live alongside them. Consequently in 1492 they decreed the expulsion from the kingdom of all Jews who would not convert to Christianity.
Although formally a religious institution as far as its members and authority were concerned, the Court of the Inquisition also had a civil side, for it was the crown who appointed and remunerated the judges and the rest of the staff. It was headed by an Inquisitor General – the first was Torquemada – and a Supreme Council. There were provincial courts – nine excluding the courts in the Americas – each of which had its attorneys, prosecutors, officials, and a large number of collaborators. The procedure for taking action was no different from that involved in the other legal institutions of the time. The accusation or proceedings taken against the accused led to his being imprisoned without knowing who had reported him or who the witnesses against him were. When the evidence was not conclusive, torture was used

to obtain a confession. The judgement given was either of acquittal or of "public reconciliation" with the accused renouncing his faith. If the accused refused to recant, he was condemned to death by burning or garroting. Judgment could be carried out publicly in an *auto–da–fé* – an intimidatory liturgical ceremony which became a mass spectacle. One of the most famous *autos* was held in Madrid in 1680 in the reign of Charles II.
The Inquisition influenced aspects of Spanish life as diverse as philosophy, science, the arts and social mores.
The museum possesses a ceramic glass tray from Toledo dating from the 16th or 17th century. In its centre is the shield of the Inquisition, with, around it, the owner's name: "Canon Pedro Sánchez de Lunar".

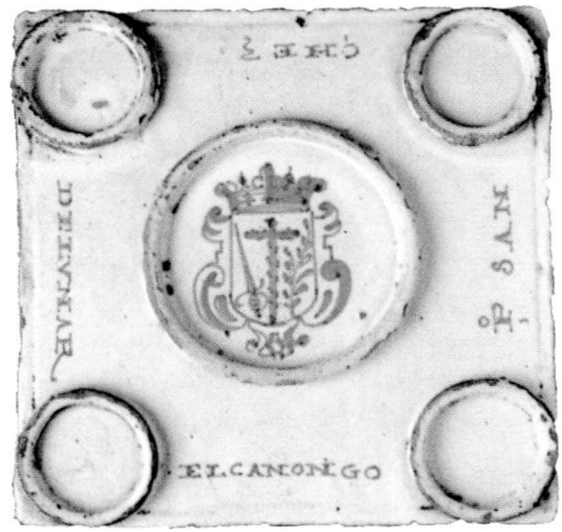

Glass tray. Ceramic. Toledo. 16th-17th century.

Excavations in the synagogue of El Tránsito

When restoration work began on the synagogue of El Tránsito, every attempt

Excavations in the east courtyard.

was made not to disturb anything connected with the building's history. Consequently, investigation was carried out in two ways:

Documentary. All the records from the various historical archives relating to the building were located and checked.

Archaeological. The excavation work was carried out by the Sephardi Museum's technical team. It was decided that digging should begin in the east courtyard under the vestibule of the present entrance. This took place between March and July of 1987. During the second phase, from 1989 to 1990, excavation of the east courtyard was completed and several probes were made in the north courtyard. The structures located were as follows:

- remains of walls under the floor of the synagogue, discovered through geophysical exploration.
- various vaulted rooms with cisterns.
- the original *hekhal* floor of monochrome glazed tiles.

The items recovered are extremely varied and cover a long period of time (10th–20th centuries). Particularly important are the coloured stuccowork fragments with Arabic inscriptions in florid Kufic script and dated as late–13th to early–14th century. Also important are the stuccowork with Hebrew characters in relief, which came from the synagogue itself, and the remains of modern and also Hispanic Muslim tiling and pottery (most of the latter dating from the 15th and 16th centuries).

The structures unearthed in the excavations provide a better idea of the synagogue of El Tránsito. It contained:

- **the ground plan and floor covering of the hekhal** (the room which contained the cabinets with the Scrolls of the Law). The room measures 4 x 6 m and the part of the floor that is still intact is of square tiles surrounded by interlocking ones with narrow rectangular black, white, green and honey–coloured glazed tiles between. The area is contemporary with the construction of the synagogue (16th century).
- **group of vaulted rooms with wells and cisterns.** These continue to the east, north and west, their main function being to collect water for communal use by the residents of the old Jewish quarter of Toledo (possibly for the public bathing establishment). They cover a long period – from the 11th to the 14th century.

Other structures, at some distance, which are also related to the synagogue of El Tránsito. These are situated at the deepest level in the cellars under the gardens of the **Casa del Greco** ("El Greco's House"). It will only be possible to draw conclusions regarding these remains after systematic excavation work has taken place.

ROOM IV

The Sephardim

The place–name *Sepharad* appears in the Bible in verse 20 of the only chapter of the book of Obadiah;

whatever its meaning in the Bible, in Hebrew it has been used, since the Middle Ages and thereafter in other languages, to refer to Spain or the Iberian Peninsula in general and to Jewish Spain in particular.
In Spanish the term *sefardí* means "a native Jew of Spain", and is correctly defined in the dictionary of the Spanish Royal Academy of Language.

The use of *sefardí* to describe by extension a Jew of mediaeval *Sefarad* according to the meaning of the word *Sephardi* in Hebrew is relatively frequent. More recently, the incorrect use of *sefardíes* has also been extended to cover Jews from Eastern countries, whether they follow the liturgical or rabbinic tradition of Sepharad or not.

Ceremonial clothing.

View of Room V.

But in Spanish the term ***sefardíes*** actually means the descendants of the Jews of Sepharad from the expulsion at the end of the Middle Ages up to the present time.

ROOM V

THE WOMEN'S GALLERY

As its name suggests, the women's gallery in the synagogue of El Tránsito is an area intended for use by the women who attended worship or meetings in the synagogue and were separated from the men. In the south wall there is a doorway (now bricked–up) which would have made it possible for the women to enter the synagogue through an entrance different from that used by the males. In spite of its vicissitudes, this large and extremely beautiful gallery still contains remains of decoration which, although rich, nevertheless does nothing to detract from the large room used by the men.
When the synagogue became the property of the knights of Calatrava and was converted into a priory and home and later into the chapel of

Stuccowork decoration in the Women's Gallery.

Nuestra Señora del Tránsito, the women's gallery was used as a dwelling. For the conversion there appears to have been no hesitation in walling up the five large windows and dividing the area up into various rooms, including a kitchen, so that it could be used as a dwelling. This caused serious damage to the stuccowork, which was completely destroyed on the west side, and partially destroyed on the south and east sides. The north wall has suffered the least damage, but smoke stains and evident attempts to remove the beautiful motifs are quite visible even today.

1) The life cycle

Birth and circumcision

"This is my covenant, which ye shall keep... Every man child among ye shall be circumcised. And ye shall circumcise the flesh of your foreskin, and it shall be a token of the covenant betwixt me and you. And he that is eight days old shall be circumcised among you, every man child in your generations... And the uncircumcised man child... that soul shall be cut off from his people; he hath broken my covenant". (Genesis 17:10–14)
The birth of a child, especially a male, is a reason for celebration in all Jewish families.
Eight days after birth, all male children must be circumcised (only in extreme cases may circumcision be postponed). The circumcision ritual is known as ***berith*** or "the covenant". Circumcision originated in the time of Abraham; its religious

Stuccowork decoration in the Women's Gallery.

Circumcision case and instruments. Silver and rock crystal. Central Europe. 19th century.

significance is that of a symbol of the covenant or agreement between God and the Jewish people.
Today circumcision is performed by an expert *mohel* ("he who circumcises") with special surgical instruments; in many cases the expert is the local Rabbi himself.
The ceremony is performed in the child's home or at the synagogue.

The ceremony must be attended by the father, the *mohel*, the godfather (*sandak*) and a group of ten adult males (*minyan*).
The day before the ceremony a special chair is placed in position. It is known as the **Chair of Elijah** because, according to tradition, the prophet Elijah is present at each circumcision, when hope of the coming of the Messiah is renewed. An adorned cloth is placed over the chair. The godfather holds the child in his lap as he sits on a high chair fitted with a footrest to facilitate the operation. Once the circumcision has been performed, the father says a prayer of thanks to God for the arrival of the new member of the community. He then blesses wine and aromatic herbs and, during the next part of the ceremony, the child is named. Prayers are then said asking for protection for the child and its mother.

If the child is a girl, she is named on the first Saturday after birth, when the father attends the synagogue for prayer. Prayers are also said for the mother and daughter.
Thirty days after the birth of the first son, the "redemption" (*pidyon*) takes place, during which the father offers the *kohen* (a descendant of

the priestly line of Aaron) silver coins which he then takes back, donating some to the synagogue for alms. The ceremony ends with blessings; one for the child and another said over a cup of wine.
This room contains a Sephardi **circumcision chair** from Jerusalem (1860). It is made of wood inlaid with ivory and there are two inscriptions in Hebrew carved on the back. The first, in the upper part reads: *Sillón de Elías el profeta* ("Chair of the Prophet Elijah"; according to tradition the prophet Elijah attends the circumcision of each male, as through this ceremony a new member is admitted into the community). Below: *Jerusalén* ("Jerusalem"). Due to the crudeness of the carving, the inscription was covered with another of gilded brass letters nailed to the wood; these were removed when the chair was restored. The word *Sión* ("Zion") is carved on the seat; it is surrounded by small ivory stars, some of which are lost. Around the lower part of the seat is a painted inscription in Hebrew: "If I forget thee, O Jerusalem, let my right hand forget her cunning. If I do not remember thee, let my tongue cleave to the roof of my mouth; if I prefer not Jerusalem above my chief joy". (Psalms 137:5–6).
The arms and back are inlaid with ivory.
Donated by the "Friends of the Sephardi Museum Association".

EDUCATION
The religious education of a Jewish boy prepares him for his place in the community to which he belongs. The mother plays a very important role in this. It is she who teaches the child respect for his elders and the most important virtues in life.

The child learns the prayers from his parents and through daily practice, all of which, together with the

Sephardic circumcision chair. Jerusalem. 20th century.

Sephardic culture.

education he receives at the synagogue school, takes him up to his "coming of religious age". The aim of this kind of education is to ensure that the child will be able to take part correctly in worship, having learned and memorized the sacred texts used in Jewish rituals. Formerly, the child attended school at a very early age, beginning to learn the Hebrew alphabet when he was four years old and continuing his studies until his majority. Having learned the alphabet, he studied the pronunciation of words and later read the Pentateuch, an event celebrated by one and all. At the rabbinic school he was taught the religious prescriptions, certain passages from the ***Talmud***, and Bible commentaries. The parents paid the rabbi, not for his tuition but for his care and vigilance of the children and to make up for the time he was unable to dedicate to his usual occupations due to teaching.
The learning method consisted of repeating, memorizing and copying the sacred texts, which enabled some

Tefillin bag. Morocco. 19th century.

Tefillin case printing blocks. Morocco. 18th-19th century.

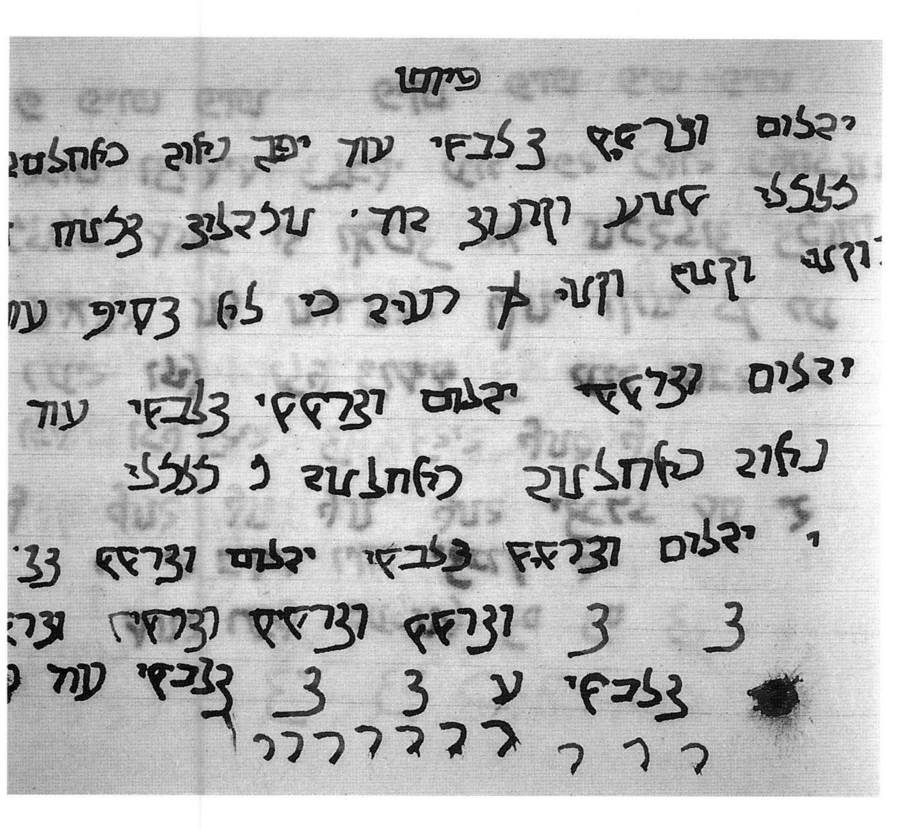

Calligraphic draft. Parchment. Tetuán. 19th century.

communities to increase the number of volumes in their libraries.

Coming of age (Bar Mitzvah)

The religious education of the male child culminates in the ceremony held at his religious majority at the age of 13. From then on he is obliged to observe the precepts (*bar mitzvah*) or religious prescriptions of Judaism and he himself (rather than his father) becomes responsible for his actions. From this time also he can form part of the quorum of ten adult males (*minyan*) that is necessary for worship.
On the days of the ceremony (a Monday or a Thursday and the preceding Saturday), the adolescent leads the service and says prayers appropriate to the occasion. He must also give a lecture (*darush*) on a passage from the Bible, drawing on the *Talmud* and *Midrash*, and comment on it. From then on the adolescent will wear the phylacteries (*tefillin*) on his forehead and left arm and cover his head with the mantle (*tallith*) at those times when its use in the synagogue is prescribed.
The synagogue ceremony ends with a party for members of the boy's family and friends to celebrate the event.
Nowadays it is customary for a ceremony to be held in the

synagogue for girls who have reached 12 years of age. This indicates that they too are subject to the precepts (*bat mitzvah*), although women are excused from many religious prescriptions.
The museum possesses a **prayer shawl bag** from Morocco dating from the 19th century.
It is embroidered with gold threads on green velvet, plant motifs and two birds which seem to evoke Psalm 84:3–4 and the yearning of the Jews for finding "rest" in Jerusalem and in the new, reconstructed Temple: "My soul longeth... for the courts of the Lord... The sparrow hath found an house, and the swallow a nest for herself, where she may lay her young". The bag also bears an embroidered abbreviated Hebrew inscription: *Shalom bar Eliahu Bothbur* ("May God keep thee and give thee life!").
On loan from the Hechal Shlomo Museum, Jerusalem.

Marriage

The wedding ceremony has two parts: the betrothal (*erusin*) and the "sanctification" (*kiddushin*) of the marriage. Formerly, the choice of partner was made by the couple's families and the wedding celebration lasted a whole week. The marriage contract (*ketubbah*), in which the bride's dowry was stipulated, was signed on a Sunday. On the same day the trousseau was displayed for qualified valuers to confirm that it fulfilled the conditions of the contract. On the Monday the bride attended the ritual bathing establishment (*mikvah*) for purification, after which she visited the groom and his family, who presented her with a **tray** with dried fruits and sugared almonds and a gift of jewels belonging to the family or purchased by the groom for the occasion. The actual wedding ceremony was always held on a Wednesday.
The ceremony takes place in the presence of at least ten adult males with the couple standing under a canopy (*huppah*). The officiating priest, generally a rabbi, pronounces the "seven benedictions" over a cup of wine. The most important part in the ceremony comes when the groom places a **ring** on the bride's finger and tells her that she is consecrated to him through the ring, in accordance with the law of Moses and Israel. By accepting the ring, the bride expresses her assent. The contract (*ketubbah*) is then publicly read, stating the groom's obligations to his wife and the compensation he will pay her in the event of divorce. The document is signed by the groom and two witnesses. The contract is kept by the bride's family as a guarantee and security for her. The ceremony ends with the groom breaking a glass with his foot, thus evoking the destruction of the Temple of Jerusalem. Formerly, the wedding celebration lasted up to seven days and was surrounded by complex ritual.
Text of a Ketubbah
Under the sign, beautiful fate and in the time of pleasure and prosperity. On Wednesday... of the month... of the year five thousand... of the creation of the world (here the equivalent year is inserted, according to the local reckoning, in this case in the city of Tetuán).

אשתך כגפן פוריה

בניך כשתילי זיתים

וראה בנים לבניך

בסימנא טבא ובמזלא יאיא ובשעת רצון ברכה רוחה והצלחה

ברביעי

Marriage contract. Tangiers. 1878.

This comely youth, Mr... the groom, of good family, son of the honourable Mr..., of good family, son of the esteemed Mr..., son of the wise and good elder Mr..., son of the knowledgeable and elder Mr..., known as..., said to the comely maid..., the bride, daughter of the wise Mr..., of good family, son of the esteemed and knowledgeable Mr..., son of the esteemed Mr..., son of the perfect sage..., happy the memory; whose surname is...: Be my wife in accordance with the law of Moses and Israel and with God's help I will sustain thee, I will maintain thee, I will clothe thee, I will give thee shelter, as Hebrew husbands sustain, maintain, clothe and shelter their wives and I will

according to custom. And this bride accepted and was his wife; and the bridegroom also accepted, and added to the dowry until reaching the

Silver and enamel pendant rings. Morocco. 20th century.

give thee the dowry of thy virginity... a zuze of silver worth... a zuze of pure silver that I must pay thee, and thy maintenance, thy clothing, and all that thou needest, and I will live together with thee

amount of... duros, a Spanish coin which circulates in this city. It was also his will to give her... by which he gave her in total... duros in the abovementioned currency; and the trousseau that the bride has

taken to the house of the bridegroom from the house of her parents including garments, jewellery and bed linen, as desired and accepted by the groom, amounts to the sum of... in the same currency, which with the dowry, the additional sum, the gift and the trousseau amount to... duros in the abovementioned currency. And the bridegroom promised not to wed any other woman except with the express consent of the bride, nor to take her out of this country to another unless it be her pleasure, and should – may God forbid – the groom wed another or take her out of this country to another without the bride's consent, he promises to pay her all that is acknowledged in this document and to give her the legal document of divorce with speed. These conditions are firm and identical to the conditions of the tribes of the children of Reuben and children of Gad. And the groom accepted responsibility for the total amount of the dowry, the supplementary amount, the gift and the trousseau and to such an effect pledged his assets both now acquired and to be acquired in the future, all in accordance with the arrangements of the scholars, not being against his will nor as a mere formality. And the groom promised with the legality prescribed by the Law, in all that is written and declared above, and with a solemn oath in the holy name of God, as do all those who swear with sincerity and without deceit, to strictly fulfil all that is written and declared in this document from its beginning to its end. All in accordance with the customs, conditions and regulations of the holy communities expelled from Castile. May God protect and have mercy on those who were saved, may He shelter them, care for them and may He who keeps the truth forever succour them. And it is under these conditions that the groom takes possession of the trousseau. And all is strong, valid and firm.

(Below, the signatures of the witnesses and the date on which the contract was signed.)

The museum possesses a pair of silver **pendant rings** from Ouazan, Morocco dating from the 19th or 20th century. These were worn by the bride at the ceremony of "cloths" which precedes the wedding. Adorned with enamel and inlaid with semi–precious stones, it is made up of two large rings from which six pendants hang in the form of small bells. These are joined by a chain with a hairpin in the middle to fix the earrings to the hair or the headdress. This one is also adorned with enamel and inlaid stones. Donated by the "Friends of the Sephardi Museum Association".

Death

Belief in life after death is a deeply–rooted aspect of the Jewish faith. As with all the ceremonies in the life cycle, everything related to death is subject to intricate ritual. The duty of burying the dead continues to be considered one of the most important in the Jewish religion and falls to the heirs of the deceased. However, for some centuries special community societies, such as the *Hevra Kaddisha* ("Holy Society"), have existed to take charge of such tasks. On receiving the news of a death, the closest relatives make a rent in their clothing (***keriah***), which is considered as an expression of resignation and mourning. The eyes of the deceased are closed by the eldest son, or, if he is unable to be present, by a relative or close friend. The corpse is then washed and the nails and hair cut. After this it is wrapped in a white linen shroud sewn with large stitches as it is intended to last only as long as the body takes to disintegrate. The use of jewellery or rich clothing as a shroud are forbidden. The body is also wrapped in the deceased's prayer shawl, the ***tallith***, whose fringes are removed or cut as the worldly is no longer of importance. The embalming of corpses is forbidden. When the body has been prepared, it is placed in a coffin and the burial rites begin. The body must be buried in virgin soil. There are no flowers at a Jewish burial. All those around the grave throw in spadefuls of earth. Once the grave has been filled, the deceased's son recites a prayer known as the *kaddish* which is similar to the

Sephardic gravestones.

Christian "Our Father". It is not customary for women to go to the cemetery. They remain at home and prepare a simple meal for the friends of the deceased and all those who have attended the burial. The food always contains egg – the symbol of life.
For the first seven days after the bereavement, the deceased's relatives must remain in mourning. They may not leave the house in which the death took place, and they must discontinue all their normal activities. They are not allowed to play games or indulge in entertainment of any kind. Relatives sit on the floor or on low seats.
The first year after the death is considered a period of mourning for the closest relatives, who go to the synagogue every day to say the *kaddish*.
Throughout the centuries Jews have wished to be buried in the Holy Land and many have travelled there to die. When such a journey is not possible they ask for a little earth from *Eretz Israel* to be placed under their heads.
In the synagogue is it customary to have "perpetual commemorative lamps". This custom, in which lamps are placed in the synagogue by the families of the deceased as an act of piety, originated in the Middle Ages.

Who would give me the talons
of a sparrowhawk!
Since my son died
I have lived in sorrow.

(Traditional Sephardic romance)
Anniversary lamp with a Hebrew inscription: "In memory of José Catito".
Morocco. 1805.
Loaned by Leticia Arbeteta of Madrid.

THE SABBATH
Saturday (*Sabbath*) is the weekly day of rest for the Jew. It begins at sunset on Friday and lasts until the same time the following day. During this period no kind of activity is permitted except that related to prayer, study of the *Torah* and acts of piety. Household tasks are forbidden so that the day can be devoted exclusively to God and the *Torah*.
The Sabbath ritual begins with the males attending evening prayer (*arbith*) at the synagogue while the women remain at home making the final preparations for the celebration. After laying the table for the meal, the wife lights two **lamps** or candles, covers her eyes with her hands and says a benediction. When the men return from the synagogue, a cup is filled with wine and the prayer of sanctification (*kiddush*) is said. The supper then begins with the *Hamotzi* benediction ("he who brings out") said over two loaves of bread (*haloth*). Sabbath food must be prepared on the eve and kept hot all through the night.
The Sabbath ends with the ceremony of the *habdalah* ("division"), in which God, who divides the sacred from the profane, light from darkness, Israel from other nations and the Sabbath from the six ordinary days, is blessed over a cup of wine. During this ceremony a benediction is also said over a box containing aromatic herbs (*besamim*), into whose aroma the

Perfume holder for the Habdalah ("Division") ceremony. Silver and ivory. Italy. 20th century.

"additional soul" of the Sabbath withdraws until the following week. A candle is then lit. Finally, those who have attended wish each other a "Good week".
The cabinet contains a table laid for the celebration of the Sabbath with a number of objects used during the ceremony:
the two **candelabra** lit by the wife to evoke the two passages from the *Torah* containing the regulations for the celebration. Bronze. 18th century. On loan from the Hechal Shlomo Museum.

Perfume holder for the ceremony of the "division" (*habdalah*). Silver and ivory. Origin unknown. 19th century.
Hebrew inscription: "He who creates all kinds of perfume." Perfume holder. On loan from the Hechal Shlomo Museum.
Kiddush **cup**. Silver. Central Europe. 20th century.
The Ferrara Bible. 16th century.

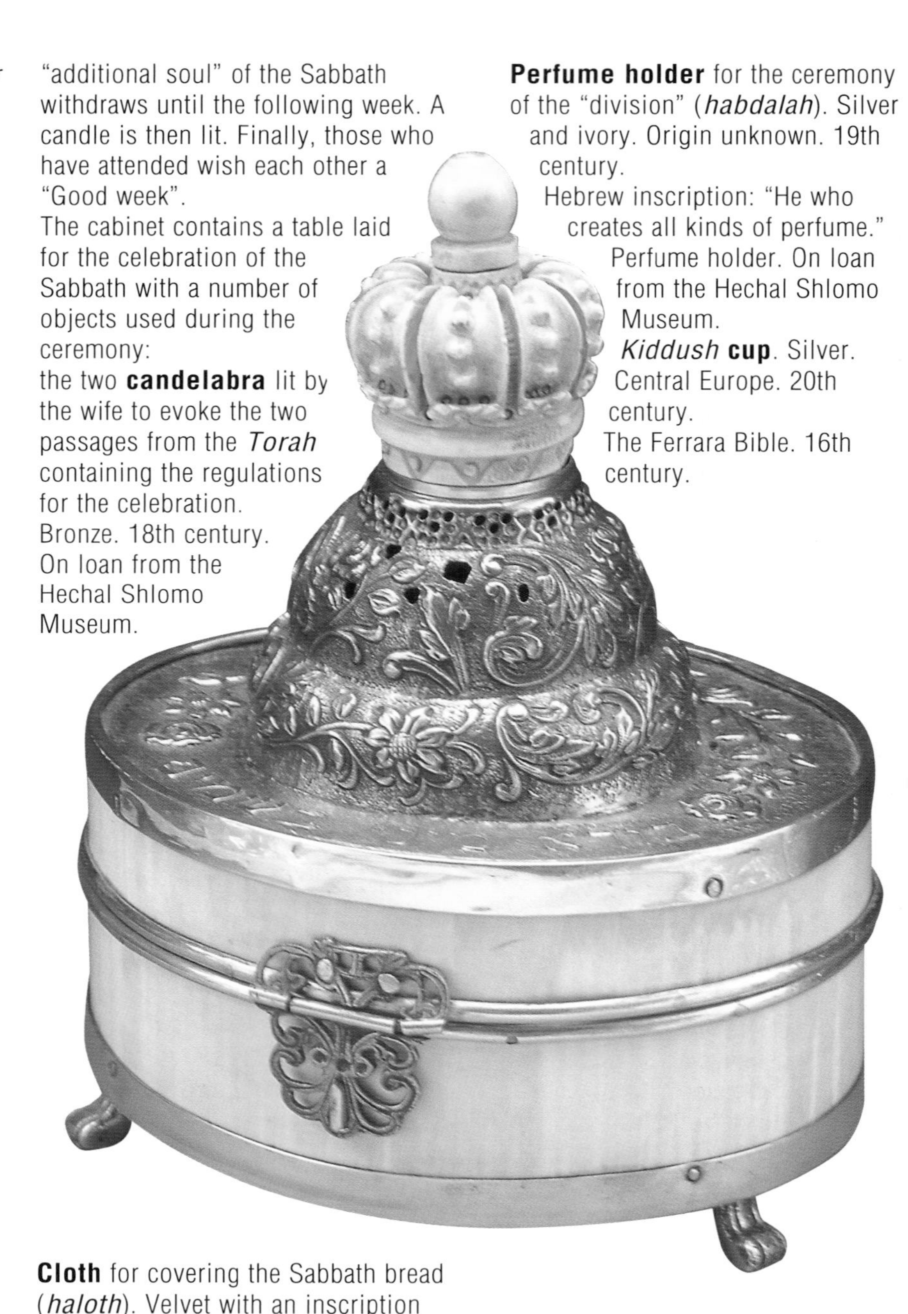

Cloth for covering the Sabbath bread (*haloth*). Velvet with an inscription painted in metallic powder. 20th century. On loan from the Hechal Shlomo Museum.

2) Annual festivals

A distinction must be made in the annual festivals between:
1) The high holy days of the "Ten Days of Penitence" (*Yamim Noraim*), which include the day of the new year (*Rosh Hoshana*) and the Day of Atonement (*Yom Kippur*).
2) The major holy days or "good days" (*Yamim Tovim*), on which it was compulsory in the time of the Temple to make a pilgrimage to Jerusalem.
These are:
Passover (*Pesah*),
Pentecost (*Shavuot*)
Tabernacles (*Sukkot*).
3) The lesser holy days recalling historical events in Jewish history:
Festival of Lights or Dedication (*Hanukkah*)
Lots (*Purim*),
15th of *Shevat* (*Tu Bi–Shevat*)
4) Those holy days on which fasting is compulsory: 9th of *Av* (*Tisha be–Av*), the day of the Destruction of the Temple.

Day of Atonement (yom Kippur)
This is the most solemn feast day in the Jewish calendar, and comes at the end of the Ten Days of Penitence (*Yamim Noraim*). It falls in September or October. From New Year (*Rosh Hoshana*) to *Yom Kippur* there are ten days of repentance and penance (*Aseret Yeme Teshuva*) during which it was customary to visit the graves of ancestors. *Yom Kippur* begins on the eve. It is a day of strict fasting on which Jews are forbidden to eat, drink, bathe, use perfume or leather footwear, have sexual relations, or, naturally, to perform any of the tasks proscribed on the Sabbath. Children are gradually accustomed to fasting, so that by the age of thirteen they are expected to do the same as their parents.
It is a solemn but not sad occasion and all worship is directed at obtaining forgiveness for the sins committed during the course of the previous year. There are curious customs connected with this holy day, such as that of Atonement (*kaparah*), on whose eve a cock is sacrificed for each male and a hen for each

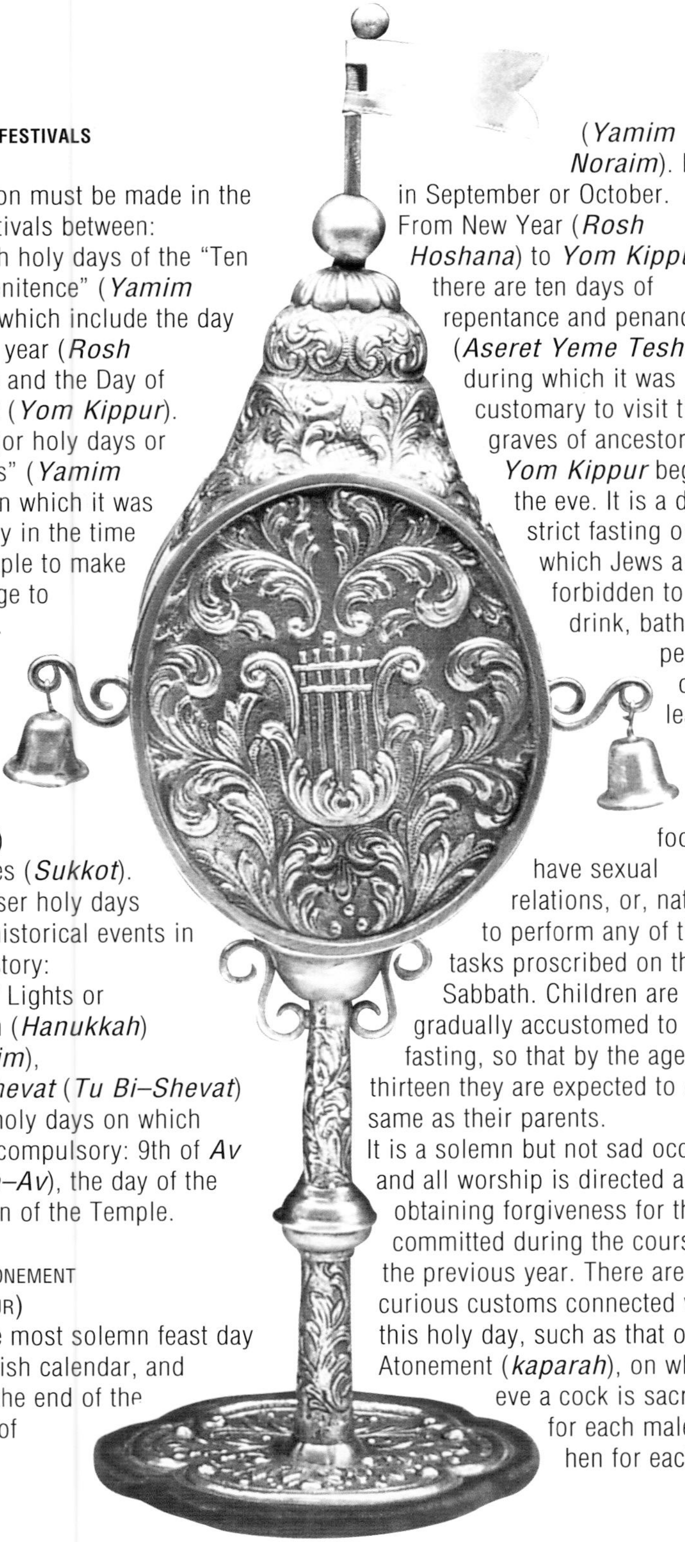

Perfume holder for the Habdalah ("Division") ceremony. Silver. Italy. 20th century.

Room V. Cabinet 2.

female as symbolic salvation. Before the fowl's throat is cut the ritual butcher (*shohet*) holds it up and describes a circle over the head of the person whose sins are to be forgiven.
The celebration begins in the synagogue with the prayer known as the ***Kol Nidre*** ("All the Vows"), the text for which is attributed to Spanish Jews during the reign of the Visigothic king Recared. Through this prayer all unfulfilled vows are nullified. Another prayer describes a divine court in which all the actions of each person are weighed. Sephardic Jews recite passages from Solomon ibn Gabirol, Jehuda ha–Levi and other Spanish Jewish poets.
The males must dress in white in remembrance of the passage from Isaiah 1:18: "Though your sins be as scarlet, they shall be as white as snow". All the cloth adornments in the synagogue are also white, and all the lamps are lit. For this occasion even non–orthodox Jews spend the whole day or most of it in the synagogue, wearing footwear associated with penitence instead of leather shoes.
Before the service ends, a ram's horn (***shofar***) is sounded to announce the end of fasting and that God has heard the prayers and has forgiven all sins.
"Also on the tenth day of this seventh month, there shall be a day of atonement: it shall be an holy convocation unto you; and ye shall afflict your souls... Ye shall do no manner of work... It shall be unto you a sabbath of rest, and ye shall afflict your souls; in the ninth day of the

Shofar or ram's horn. Tetuán. 19th century.

month at even, from even unto even, shall ye celebrate your sabbath". (Leviticus 23:27–32)

THE FEAST OF TABERNACLES OR SUKKOT

The Feast of Tabernacles or Booths (*Sukkot*) is celebrated over a period of eight days, between the 15th and the 22nd of *Tishri* (in September or October). It commemorates the time after the people of Israel left Egypt and wandered in the desert, living in simple tents; this celebration was established with another – the grape and crop harvest festival. In remembrance of both, each family must build a booth (*sukkah*), where it is customary to make all meals for the duration of the festival. The *sukkah* must be a small, temporary structure with at least three walls; the roof must be covered with branches and leaves protecting it from the sunlight but allowing the stars to be seen. It must be furnished like the house itself and adorned with produce associated with the countryside – flowers, fruit, garlands, etc. To these, tapestries, pictures, paper chains, lanterns, and anything else considered relevant may be added. Some *sukkot* are veritable works of art.

In the synagogue, agricultural products of a symbolic nature are used. A citron (*etrog*) is held in the left hand and a palm branch (*lulav*) bound with three myrtle (*hadas*) and two willow branches (*arava*) is held in the right. The branch is waved to east, south, west and north three times and then up and down. The citrons (*etrogim*) are kept in artistic **cases** made of silver or some other rare material and are characterized by their beautiful ornamentation.

According to tradition, seven important guests (*ushpizin*) visit the *sukkah* during the festival: Abraham, Isaac, Jacob, Joseph, Moses, Aaron, and David; an **engraving** or **plaque** on the *sukkah* wall bears their names. The guest for each particular day is invited to attend in a prayer said over the meal. During the festival it is customary to read Ecclesiastes (*Koheleth*) as a contrast to the festive air of this time.

An important ceremony during this period is that in which God is asked to send rain for the coming winter. At the end of *Sukkot* the "Rejoicing

Citron case (etrog). Silver. Italy. 19th century.

Hanukkah lamp. Bronze. Morocco. 20th century.

of the Law" (*Simhat Torah*) is celebrated, when the Law as revealed by God to His chosen people is praised. The occasion is celebrated with great displays of happiness during which, to singing and dancing, the scrolls of the Law are borne in procession around the reading desk (*tevah*) seven times. The central figures in this celebration are the "bridegroom of the Law" (*Hatan Torah*) and the "bridegroom of the Genesis" (*Hatan Bereshit*), who read the last and the first parts of the sacred text in a ritual reminiscent of a wedding ceremony.

Rattle. Ivory. Mediterranean area. Hebrew inscription: "Damned Haman".

The previous page features a beautiful **citron container,** or *etrog*, from Italy, c. 1800. Made of silver, the *etrog* is used during the Festival of Booths to contain the citron, one of the items used during worship in the synagogue. The upper part or cover is engraved and fretted with vegetal motifs (acanthus leaves). At the top is an open flower. The lower part contains acanthus leaves greater in detail. The balustered support rests on a square base.

THE FEAST OF LIGHTS (HANUKKAH)

This feast, which falls at the end of the month of Kislev (December), lasts for eight days. It commemorates the rededication of the Temple of Jerusalem in 165 B.C., after the Maccabees defeated the Greek Antiochus Epiphanes, who had forbidden the worship of God in the Temple and, in an attempt to oblige the Jews to adopt Hellenistic customs and culture, decreed that it should be dedicated to Zeus instead.

The use of light during this time recalls a

pious legend in Jewish tradition which took place when, on relighting the lamp of the Holy of Holies, it was discovered that there was not enough consecrated oil for more than one day; however, in spite of this the light remained lit and on the eighth day the Jewish revolt ended in victory. In commemoration of this event, the festival lasts for eight days; each night an additional light is lit in a *Hanukkah lamp* with eight receptacles for wicks and oil (plus a ninth) until by the eighth night all have been lit.

Children are at the centre of this festival: they are given coins or other gifts and play with a teetotum (*sevivon*) whose four sides bear Hebrew letters forming the sentence "A great miracle occurred there".

The lamp must be placed near a window so that its light will indicate to passersby that the household is Jewish.

The **Hanukkah lamp** on display in the museum is of gilded metal, comes from Morocco, and was made in the 19th century. It has a number of lobed containers, each with a five–pointed star above, and there is a hole for hanging the lamp. A double circle contains a theme taken from Numbers 13:23: "And they came unto the brook of Eshcol, and cut down from thence a branch with one cluster of grapes, and they bare it between two upon a staff..."

Below, eight receptacles for wicks (plus one more in the upper part) and drip catchers.

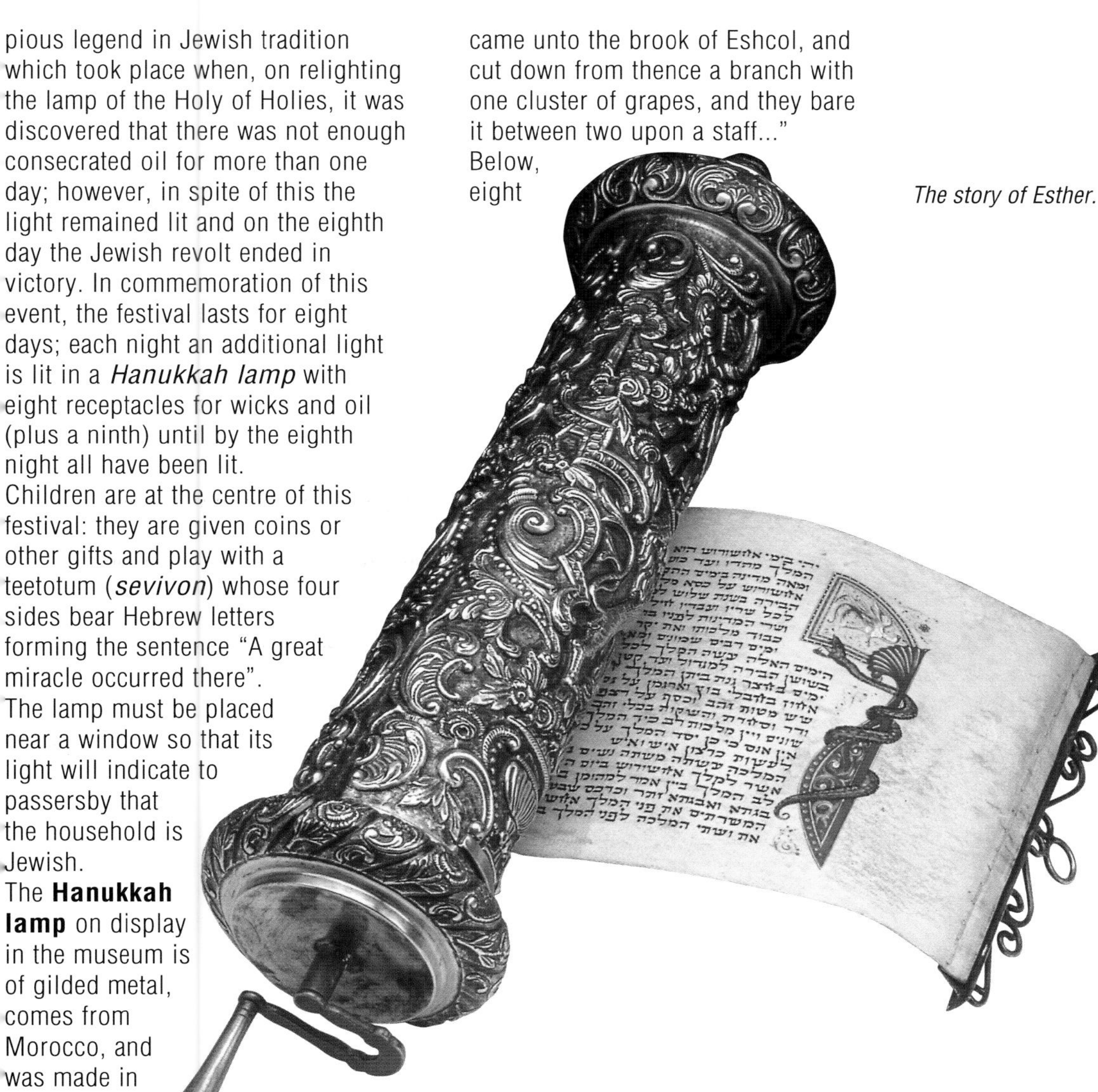

The story of Esther.

THE FEAST OF LOTS (PURIM)

The feast of Lots (*Purim*) is celebrated on the 14th of *Adar* (February–March) and commemorates the miraculous salvation of the Jews of Persia

thanks to the intercession of Queen Esther and her uncle Mordecai. Counting on the favour of the Persian king (Xerxes or Artaxerxes), the courtier Haman accused the Jews of not obeying the laws of the kingdom as their laws were different from those of the other peoples, and cast lots to see on which day they should die. When Mordecai heard of this, he told the queen, who spoke to the king and so managed to save her people; Haman and his ten children were hanged. The story is told in detail on a scroll (*megillah*) read in Hebrew in the synagogue during the evening and morning services, while the congregation follow the passage with small rolls of their own (*megilloth*) and the children whistle and sound **rattles** in derision each time the name of the wicked Haman is uttered.
The decoration on these scrolls can be extremely rich and varied, as lay motifs are permitted – which has fired the imagination of many writers and illuminators. The story of Esther and depictions of her according to each country and age, scenes of gallantry, flowers, fruit, etc., are only a few of the themes which adorn the *megilloth*. They also contain burlesque motifs with Haman as the central character.
During this feast, it is permitted to drink to the point of confusing the names of Mordecai and Haman, and sweet things are eaten; alms are given to the poor and money, dishes of sweets, clothes and jewellery are given to friends and relatives, especially to children. Also common at this time are plays, games of chance and dressing up in costumes (the origin of modern theatre). *Purim* is, in fact, the Jewish "carnival"; adults and children alike don costumes, the festival is celebrated with great merrymaking and even the rabbis and students of the rabbinic school join in.
***Megillah* Scroll of Esther.** Italy. 20th century.
It contains the history of Esther in 20 columns on parchment. The silver repoussé case is adorned with exquisite geometric, plant and animal motifs. The cylinder has a handle for winding the parchment on, making reading easier.
All the initial letters at the beginning of each column are larger in size than the rest of the text and are coloured – red, green, blue and gold. The first letter on the scroll is artistically adorned with a coiled serpent while the top part has a kind of fan from which the horizontal line of the letter begins. Here there is a fantastic animal with the body of a bird with exuberant plumage and the head of a deer. Other decorative motifs are included at the end and before the list of those killed by the Jews (Esther 8:5-10).

THE FEAST OF THE PASSOVER (PESAH)

Passover (in biblical times, one of the three feasts of pilgrimage to the Temple of Jerusalem) is celebrated over eight days in April from 15th-23rd of Nisan. Its origin is lost in time, as it was once a holy day for shepherds to which another (agricultural) festival was added, during which it was forbidden to eat

or possess bread or any other food containing yeast. Subsequently it became a festival of freedom commemorating the Jews' release from slavery in Egypt, as is told in the Book of Exodus. The flight from Egypt is remembered each year during the "order" (*Seder*) on the first two nights of Passover, when each family dines at home and the *Haggadah* (the narration in Hebrew of the exodus according to the rabbinic texts), is read.

On the days prior to the Passover, the Jewish household must be thoroughly cleaned in order to eliminate any food containing leavening agents from utensils and garments, for according to the Bible the Jews left Egypt in such a hurry

Items used during the Feast of Passover. On loan from the Hechal Shlomo Museum, Jerusalem.

Detail of a Passover cloth. Painted. 18th century.

that there was not enough time for the dough to rise. A specific ritual dictates the procedure to follow both with such foods and the containers that have held them, and it is customary to keep a special dinner

service for use only during Passover. The main function of the *Seder* is to relive the exodus and to make children understand the miraculous event which took place in the lives of their ancestors. The most important

Detail of a Passover cloth. Painted. 18th century.

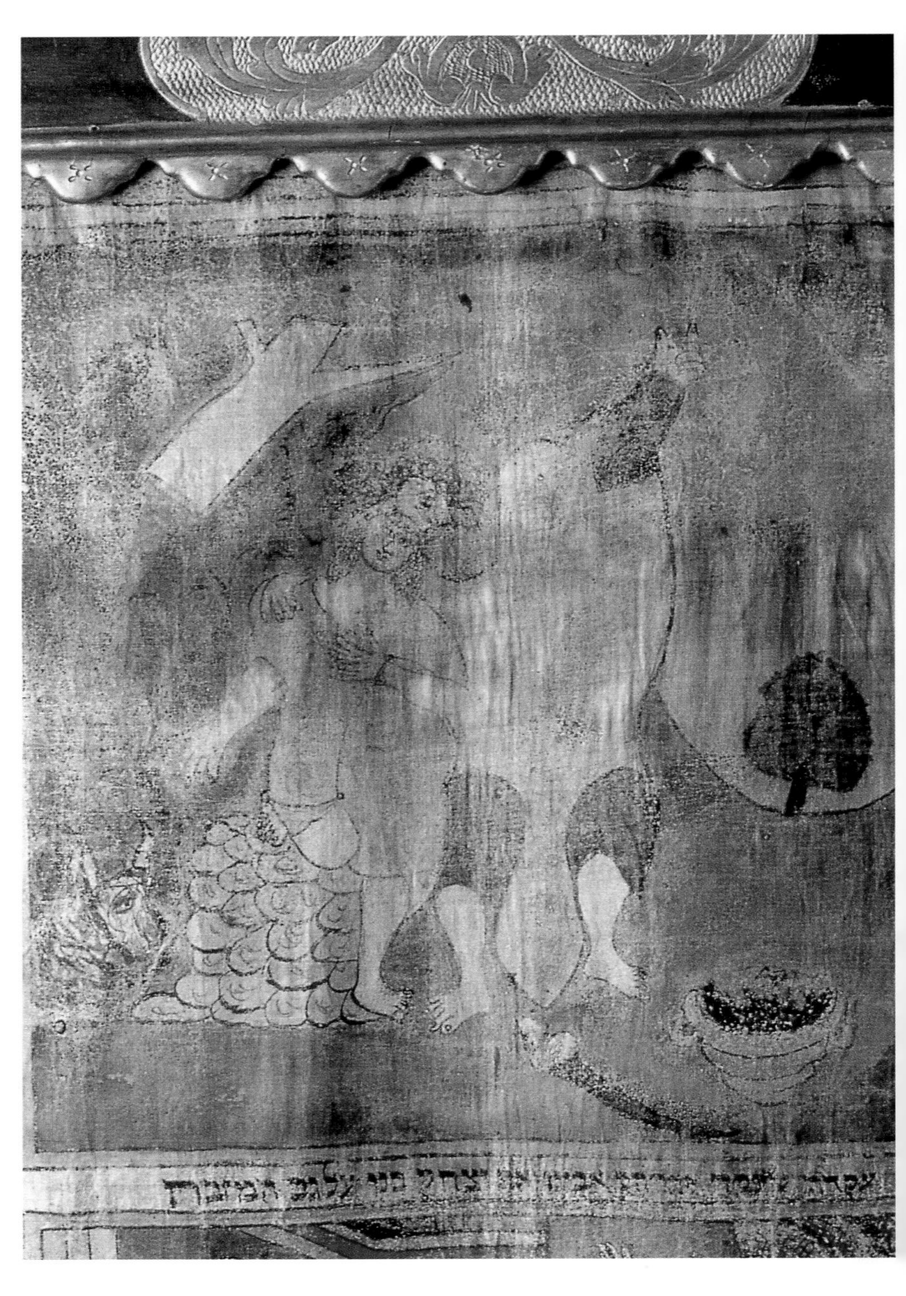

Detail of a Passover cloth. Painted. 18th century.

moment comes almost at the beginning of the *Haggadah* reading when the youngest son in the house (or if there are no sons, the mother) exclaims: "*How different this night is from all other nights!*"

Detail of a Passover cloth. Painted. 18th century.

For the meal a special **dish** is prepared. This contains several foods that must be eaten during the *Seder* and which symbolise the hardships and suffering of the Jews in Egypt and the miraculous intervention of

God on behalf of His chosen people. These are:

three loaves of unleavened bread (*matzoth*), one on top of another, symbolising the three groups of Jews – the priests, the Levites and the rest of the people.

bitter herbs (*maror*), such as lettuce, endives, radishes, watercress, etc., symbolising the bitterness of slavery.

a paste (*haroset*), made with ground fruit, cinnamon, honey, apple and wine, recalling the mortar used in Egypt for Pharaoh's buildings.

a shank bone (*zeroa*) of lamb, representing the outstretched arm of God who freed the children of Israel from slavery.

celery (*karpas*), the first bitter herb dipped in a container holding vinegar or salt water.

a hard-boiled egg (*betzah*), typical of mourning, symbolising the fleetingness of the worldly and alluding to the pain caused by the destruction of the Temple of Jerusalem.

a container with salt water or vinegar in which to dip the *karpas*, recalling the waters of the Red Sea, crossed by the Israelites in their flight from Egypt.

During the celebration each person at the table must have a *Haggadah*, the book containing the story of the exodus, as it is read during the meal. It is in fact a sort of manual in Hebrew for the *Seder* and is often translated into other languages.

During the meal four cups of wine are blessed and drunk. The meaning of this is explained in the Bible and the *Talmud*. One cup of wine recalls God's promise of redemption to Israel as expressed in four verbs in the first person (Exodus 6:6-7: "...I will bring you out ...I will rid you of their bondage ...I will redeem you ...I will take you to me".

The photographs on the four previous pages are of an **ornamental Passover cloth** made in Germany in 1856.

It was used as a decorative element for Passover. Painted in soft tones on this fine cloth are a number of motifs connected with the feast which at the same time serve as a record of the various stages in the meal. The purpose of the scenes is to show God's mercy for His people, whom He saved from slavery in Egypt.

The centre contains seven large scenes with:

the sacrifice of Isaac
Joseph presented to his brothers and embracing Benjamin
the meeting between Joseph and his father, Jacob
the crossing of the Red Sea
Moses receiving the *Torah* on Mount Sinai
Temple furniture
meditation and study.

On the left-hand side, thirteen vignettes depict the most important moments of the *Seder*. On the left, in ten vignettes, the plagues with which the Egyptians were afflicted for not allowing the Israelites to leave Egypt. The four cups of wine that are drunk during the *Seder* recall God's four promises of hope and redemption to his people – "I will redeem you", "I will take you to me, I will bring you out, ...I will rid you of their bondage". The four types of

person who ask questions about the celebration reflect different attitudes toward it, and Moses, Aaron, David and Solomon complete the sets of four. In the lower part the sentence: "If you forget Jerusalem...", the date (year 56) and the author, Isaac Iager. On loan from the Museum of Santa Cruz, Toledo.

THE SEPHARDIC LANGUAGE

The long centuries of co-existence in mediaeval Sepharad left Sephardic Judaism impregnated with a number of Hispanic features, the most noteworthy being in the language spoken by Jews.
The origin of the Sephardic language lies in the Castilian of the times of the expulsion. Like all living languages, it has evolved over the centuries, being subject to the influence of other languages and internal development, until finally becoming an independent language, close to but different from the Spanish spoken in Spain and Latin America.
For more than four centuries the Sephardic language was an effective instrument not only of oral communication but also of literary expression for the Sephardim, for apart from the oral transmission of traditional literature, the Sephardic language also produced important cultivated literature written by individual authors which saw its golden age in the 18th century. For historical and social reasons the number of Sephardic speakers has fallen in the last few generations to the lowest number ever.
Usually known by philologists as Judaeo-Spanish, it has also been called *Jidió, Judesmo* or *Español* in the east and *Jaquetía* in the area

A sephardic family.

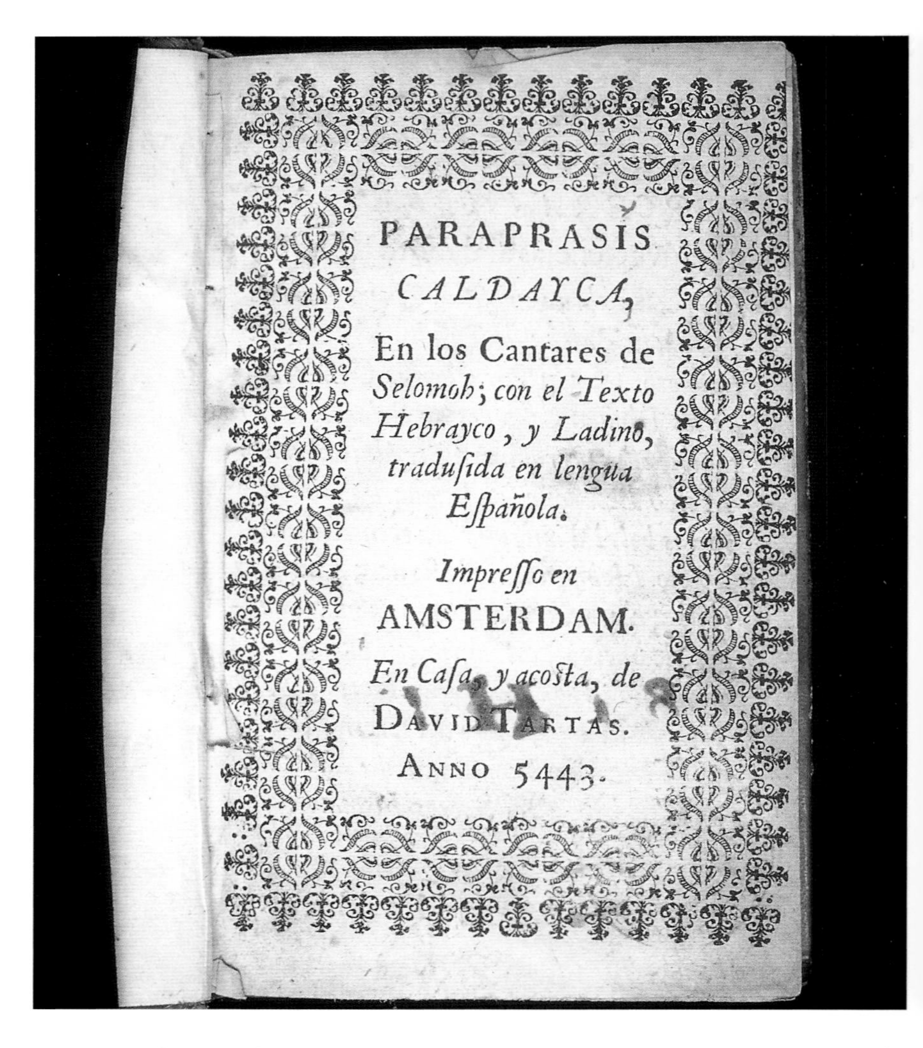

PARAPRASIS
CALDAYCA,
En los Cantares de
Selomoh; con el Texto
Hebrayco, y Ladino,
tradusida en lengua
Española.

Impresso en
AMSTERDAM.
En Casa, y acosta, de
DAVID TARTAS.
ANNO 5443.

Sephardic language.

around the Strait of Gibraltar. It is sometimes called *Ladino*, the term used in the Hebrew spoken in Israel. However, strictly speaking *Ladino* is a specific mode of the Sephardic language used in traditional teaching and in the liturgy for translating the sacred texts from Hebrew and Aramaic. Thus *Ladino* is characterized by remaining extremely close to these original texts, which in turn has led to the sacred language translated being projected onto Sephardic.

SEPHARDIC LITERATURE

Sephardic literature spanned several centuries and lasted while those conditions which made it possible existed, i.e. a network of communities whose language served as a means not only of oral and written communication but also of literary expression. The 18th century saw a golden age in Sephardic literature. Virtually all the production of the early centuries (and almost certainly the most traditional) developed highly Jewish themes. But after a process of modernization and secularization in the middle of the 19th century, the language opened up to European

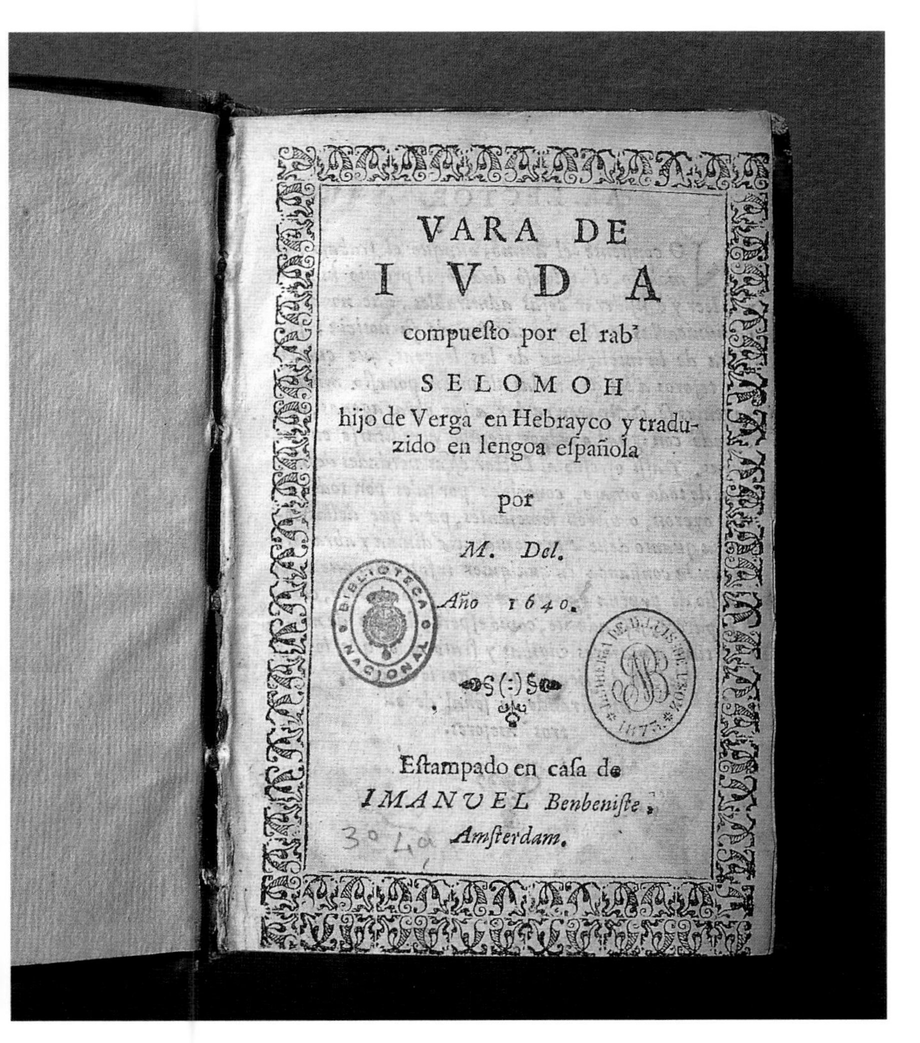
VARA DE
I V D A
compueſto por el rab.
SELOMOH
hijo de Verga en Hebrayco y tradu-
zido en lengoa eſpañola
por
M. Del.
Año 1640.

Eſtampado en caſa de
IMANVEL Benbeniſte,
Amſterdam.

Sephardic literature.

cultural currents and adopted new, universal genres.

Works on the Jewish heritage are based on the beliefs and values which make up the spiritual, mental and experiential world of traditional Judaism. They are collections of prayers, biblical commentaries, moral treatises, religious regulations, tales of piety, etc.

Where prose is concerned, the vast work known as *Me'am Lo'ez* is particularly important. Begun in 1732 by Jacob Culi, various authors continued working on it for almost two centuries more and it was constantly republished. Structured as a linear commentary of the Bible interspersed with more or less related themes, it recounts the whole of traditional Jewish knowledge in a way both interesting for the reader and suitable for those without access to Hebrew sources.

The *coplas* are the Sephardim's truest and most traditional poetic manifestation. The several hundred verse poems of different lengths and with a uniform metre have specifically Sephardic, if not generally Jewish, themes, while in form they develop certain characteristics present in mediaeval Spanish poetry.

Among the genres adopted belatedly from other literatures, particularly important are narrative and theatre, which became very popular from the middle of the 19th century. An important vehicle in the spread of the new literary aesthetics was journalism, whose development was notable.

As well as the cultivated literature written by individual authors, the Sephardim have amply developed, and to a certain extent continue to develop, the traditional genres of oral transmission, such as the *romancero* (collection of ballads) and the *cancionero* (anthologies), both in verse, as well as the *cuento* (short story) and the *refrán* (saying) in prose. These genres have been studied in the greatest detail and are consequently the best-known. However, this has led some people who knew nothing of the literature written over the centuries to believe that the only Sephardic literature is that which has been transmitted orally. Such ignorance may well be explained by the fact that although this literature was expressed in a Hispanic language, until relatively recently it was mainly written down in *aljamía*, i.e. with letters from the Hebrew alphabet, giving rise to the impression that the language used was Hebrew.

Elsewhere, the literary works of Sephardim in Italy and the Netherlands have formed part of the Spanish Sephardic literature of the golden age.

JEWS IN MODERN AND CONTEMPORARY SPAIN

As early as the 17th century the Count-Duke of Olivares considered allowing Jews to return to Spain in order to stimulate the economy. However this was incompatible with an Inquisition intent on forbidding any form of religious or ideological pluralism. As late as 1802 a royal decree repeated the "orders and decisions concerning what must be done with the Jews who have arrived and will arrive" in Spain (almost certainly using Gibraltar as a bridgehead). With the abolition of the Inquisition in 1834, however, the situation began to change.
When Spanish troops – and with them reporters and writers – entered Tetuán on 6th February 1860 during the war in Africa, they came upon a community of Sephardim who spoke to them in their own language. Castelar's speeches in the Constituent Assembly were the first assessment of these Jews as being Spanish; and the constitution of 1869 abolished the old expulsion edict. At this time the first Jewish settlements began to appear on the Spanish mainland (Cadiz and Seville), although others already existed in the Spanish colonies in North Africa (Ceuta and Melilla). This coincided with the first studies of Spanish Jews (Amador de los Ríos, Fidel Fita), and a new interest in the subject on the part of writers (Galdós, etc.) and intellectuals.

At the turn of the century, Senator Ángel Pulido promoted a campaign in favour of the Sephardim; subsequently the Hispano-Hebrew Association was founded, and in 1924 a royal decree granted naturalization papers to members of ancient protected Sephardic families who fulfilled certain consular requirements.
During the Second Republic, freedom of worship led to the opening of oratories and to an increase in the Jewish communities of Madrid and Barcelona with the arrival of Sephardic and Ashkenazic Jewish immigrants. During the Spanish Civil War, of the Jews resident in Spain some fought on the side of the Republic, while others supported Franco; to the first group we must add the noteworthy participation of Jews in the International Brigades.

The Synagogue in Madrid.

The scant official initiative on the part of the Spanish government regarding the deportation of Jews during World War II contrasts sharply with the exemplary – at times heroic – action of certain diplomats who issued Sephardim with documents which effectively saved their lives.
In 1954 the first completely new synagogue to be built since the expulsion opened in Barcelona; others were subsequently opened in Madrid (1968) and Marbella, among other cities. In the 1960s Jews came to Spain from North Africa and in subsequent decades new communities formed a Federation. Immigration continues, mainly from Spanish America (Southern cone). The Spanish constitution of 1978 acknowledged the members of the new Jewish community of Spain as full citizens. The awarding of the "Prince of Asturias Prize" to the Sephardic communities in 1990 came as a prelude to the commemoration of the half millennium since the expulsion (*Sefarad 92*), culminating in the visit by the King and Queen of Spain to the synagogue of Madrid (also in 1992).
In addition to these historic occasions, the following events have also been particularly important as far as culture is concerned: the celebration of the VIII centenary of the birth of Maimonides (1935); the creation at the CSIC (1940) of the "'Arias Montano' Institute of Hebrew Studies" and its magazine *Sefarad*, and of chairs and departments of Hebrew at a number of universities; the "World Sephardic Bibliographical Exhibition" (1959), the consequent creation of the "Institute of Sephardic Studies" and shortly after that of the "Sephardi Museum" (1964); the organisation, from the mid-80s on, of a large number of courses, congresses and other academic events, as well as a proliferation of publications on various aspects of Spanish and Sephardic Judaism; the major exhibition "Jewish Life in Sefarad" (1992); and finally – or at least for the moment – the reopening of the remodelled Sephardi Museum.

Restoration work on the Synagogue of El Tránsito.

BIBLIOGRAPHY

ABRAHAM, I. *Jewish Life in the Middle Ages*, New York, A Temple Book Atheneum, 1981.

AMADOR DE LOS RÍOS, J. *Historia de los judíos de España y Portugal...* Madrid, T. Fortamet, 1875, 3 vols.

BAER, Y. *Los judíos en la España cristiana*, revised by J. L. Lacave, Madrid, Altalena, 1981. 2 vols.

CANTERA BURGOS, Francisco. *Sinagogas españolas*, Madrid, CSIC, 1956. By the same author: *Sinagogas de Toledo, Segovia y Córdoba*, CSIC, Madrid, 1973.

CANTERA, F. and MILLÁS VALLICROSA, J. María. *Las inscripciones hebraicas de España*, Madrid, CSIC, 1955.

CHILL, Abraham. *The Minhagim, the Customs and Ceremonies of Judaism, their Origins and Rationale*, New York, 1979.

DELGADO VALERO, Clara. *Toledo Islámico: ciudad, arte e historia*, Toledo, Caja de Ahorros de Toledo, 1987.

DÍAZ-MAS Paloma. *Los sefardíes. Historia, lengua y cultura*, Barcelona, Riopiedras, 1986.

FISHMAN, Priscila. *Minor and Modern Festivals*, Jerusalem, 1973.

GARCÍA MORENO, Luis A. *Los judíos de la España Antigua*, Madrid, Rialp, 1993.

IDELSOHN, A. Z. *Jewish Liturgy and its Development*, 2nd ed., New York, 1972.

KANOF, Abram. *Jewish Ceremonial Art and Religious Observance*, New York, 1969.

LACAVE, José Luis. *Juderías y sinagogas españolas*, Madrid, Mapfre, 1992.

LACAVE, José Luis, ARMENGOL, M., ONTAÑÓN, F. *Sefarad, Sefarad, La España judía.* Barcelona, Lunwerg, 1987.

LEÓN TELLO, P. *Judíos de Toledo*, Madrid, CSIC, 1979, 2 vols.

LÓPEZ ÁLVAREZ, Ana María. *Catálogo del Museo Sefardí*, Madrid, Ministerio de Cultura, 1987.

LÓPEZ ÁLVAREZ, Ana María, PALOMERO PLAZA, S., MENÉNDEZ ROBLES, María Luisa. *Guía del Museo Sefardí*, Salamanca, 1994.

LÓPEZ ÁLVAREZ, Ana María, IZQUIERDO BENITO, R., PALOMERO PLAZA, S. *Guía del Toledo judío*, Madrid, 1990.

MOLHO, Michael. *Usos y costumbres de los Sefardíes de Salónica*, Madrid. CSIC, 1950.

NAVARRO PEIRO, Ángeles. *Literatura hispanohebrea (siglos X-XIII)*, Córdoba,

El Almendro, 1988.

PELÁEZ DEL ROSAL, Jesús. *Los judíos y Lucena, Córdoba*, El Almendro, 1988.

PELÁEZ DEL ROSAL, Jesús. *The Jews in Cordoba, Córdoba*, El Almendro, 1982.

PÉREZ HIGUERA, Teresa. *Paseos por el Toledo del siglo XIII, Alfonso X*, Madrid. Ministerio de Cultura, 1984.

PORRES MARTíN-CLETO, Julio. *Historia de las calles de Toledo*, 2nd ed. Toledo, 1982.

POSNER, Raphael et al. *Jewish Liturgy: Prayer and Synagogue...*, Jerusalem, 1975.

Raíces judías en España (various authors). Madrid, Iberia, 1988.

ROMANO, David. *La ciencia hispanojudía*, Madrid, Mapfre, 1992.

ROMERO CASTELLO, E. *La vida judía en Sefarad*, Sinagoga del Tránsito. Toledo, November 1991- January 1992. Madrid, Ministerio de Cultura, 1991.

ROMERO CASTELLO, E. and MACÍAS KAPON, U. *Los judíos de Europa. Un legado de 2000 años*. Madrid, Anaya, 1994.

SÁENZ-BADILLOS, A., TARGARONA BORRÁS, J. *Diccionario de autores judíos (Sefarad. Siglos X-XV)*, Córdoba, El Almendro, 1988.

SÁENZ-BADILLOS, A. *Literatura hebrea en la España medieval*, Madrid, Amigos de Sefarad, 1991.

SUÁREZ FERNÁNDEZ, Luis. *Judíos españoles en la Edad Media*, Madrid, Rialp, 1980.

WIGODER, Geoffrey. *Art et civilisation du peuple juif*, Paría, S.A.